Hawai'i Cooks
From the Garden

Maili Yardley

Mutual Publishing

Other books by the author

HAWAIʻI'S GLAMOUR DAYS
KITCHEN SCRIPTURE
HAWAIʻI COOKS
HAWAIʻI COOKS THE ISLAND WAY
HAWAIʻI COOKS THROUGHOUT THE YEAR
HAWAIʻI TIDES AND TIMES
AUNTIE POEPE
THE HISTORY OF KAPIʻOLANI HOSPITAL
THE HISTORY OF KAUIKEOLANI CHILDREN'S HOSPITAL
HOW THE ANT FAMILY CAME TO HAWAII

First Printing May 1997
97 98 99 00 01 02

ISBN 1-56647-131-1

Design by Kennedy and Preiss Graphic Design

Mutual Publishing
1127 11th Avenue, Mezz. B
Honolulu, Hawaii 96816
Telephone (808) 732-1709
Fax (808) 734-4094
e-mail: mutual@lava.net

Dedication

And God said, "Behold, I have given you every plant yielding seed
which is upon the face of all the earth, and every tree with seed in its fruit you
shall have them for food."
Genesis 1:29

Table of Contents

Introduction

How well I remember a day sometime in 1921… We were living in a small cottage on Spreckels Street (named for the California baron, Claus Spreckels, whose three-storied mansion once sat on property facing Wilder Avenue and Punahou Street) and my father came home and announced to my mother and me that he had bought a house on Pensacola Street. He paid $25,000 for an acre of land, a rambling house with separate wash house, a one-bedroom caretaker's cottage and a barn for the cows and a horse.

The house itself had a welcoming lanai, with comfortable seating areas of wicker furniture along the front, a living room large enough for my mother's cherished Steinway grand piano, a dining room with adjoining fernery, a den where we kids had great fun pumping on the old organ, a huge kitchen and a back porch where we ate breakfast and lunch. The wooden icebox sat conveniently by the back door so the pail of melted ice water could be thrown out once a day, and a screened food safe, with its four legs set in cans of water to deter the ants, stood nearby. The rest of the house consisted of bedrooms and a screened porch for the family and two live-in help.

The help situation needed for this larger home was eased considerably by the Salvation Army. The Army maintained headquarters at the end of Manoa Valley, where orphans and other children lived and were trained in the adjoining bakery that turned out tempting pastries and breads. Some of the boys and girls were willing to work in homes for keep and a small salary. That is where my mother found Rachel and Mary, who worked in the house, and Peter, who lived in rooms off the wash house for almost 15 years and left with a sizable nest egg my mother had saved for him.

Soon thereafter, I remember my father instructing Peter one fine morning to take me up in the mango tree, which was no easy task for someone so plump! Poor Peter, he had a tough challenge getting me up and then staying put until my father called for us to come down. He took my hand and led me into their bedroom and introduced me to a small bundle lying beside my mother. Miss Crowe, the nurse, Dr. John Milnor, my father, my mother… they were all ecstatically beaming! And at that moment I realized my life was changing! I now had competition after being the lone star in a lovely world for seven years.

Like most *kamaʻaina* homes, the yard consisted of sprawling patches of lawn, plots of flowers and various flowering and fruit trees. A horseshoe driveway led to the front steps and a continuation on the *makai* side led to the garage and back area. This narrow strip was planted with strawberry guava bushes that were always pruned low to provide us with delicious fruit. How I loved standing under those branches and picking off an attractive fruit to consume.

Three towering mango trees dominated the front yard... one on the *mauka* side of the property and the others hung over the driveway to the rear. It was my job... and how I hated it... to pick up all the fallen mangoes before any car drove out from the garage. So now, whenever I see a crushed mango in the road, I'm taken back to those dreary days when I could so easily have come to hate mangoes... but I still love those luscious fruit.

Along the *mauka* side of the property were several varieties of fruit trees... pomelos that seemed to hang there just sagging under their own weight, a gnarled orange, an unpruned surinam cherry tree and a mangosteen with its dagger-like thorns and bright-yellow fruit that was so sour we never bothered to pick them. Today, the mangosteen has become quite rare and very seldom do you see one.

When we took over the property, the cows and horse were no more, but the fence that divided the property in half still stood and the cumbersome gates were left open. The barn was converted into a rather intriguing home by two enterprising bachelor friends of the family. There was a large living room with steps down to two bedrooms and up to a studio in the loft. A bath and kitchen were installed on the cement portion formerly used for milking. The cottage was let out as an attractive rental to very special tenants.

Peter tended the vegetable garden that provided our table with the freshest of produce, and I had my own little patch where I watched the radishes and carrots grow but never fast enough for my youthful enthusiasm. There were papaya trees for fresh fruit on the table every morning and delicate creamy flowers to make leis when we were so inclined. The fig trees were usually draped in old mosquito netting so that the birds wouldn't get to the fruit first. I especially loved to hunt for the rosy-red sweet, small tomatoes abounding in the mounds of spreading branches that grew wild. It was great sport to pick and pop in the mouth while still warm, but my mother coveted them for her dishes of lomi salmon, always contending they were far superior to regular tomatoes in that particular dish.

In the farthest corner of the backyard was the fire pit... a thing unheard of today... where all the trash and large cuttings were burned. Cans and bottles were left for the garbage man. Nearby was the laundry line, so there were definitely designated times for burning and drying. As I look back on those days, I marvel that the wash house was so inconveniently located that poor Mary had to *hapai* the heavy baskets of laundry quite a distance.

In those days laundry was done in two large stationary side-by-side tubs. First the clothes were soaked in soapy water, then scrubbed on the worn wooden washboard and rinsed in a tub of clear water, and anything that had to be bleached was simply thrown on the lawn before rinsing in new water and left in the sun to whiten. If there were stubborn stains, these were treated with lemon and Hawaiian salt and thrown on the grass again to whiten.

Starch had to be cooked in the kitchen and carted to the tubs and added to a little water for the clothes to be dipped in. All the linen hand towels, pillow cases, napkins, tablecloths and some clothes, including my father's cotton shirts, had to be starched and hung on the line to dry. Then they were sprinkled with water, neatly rolled up and stacked in a pile to be ironed. Fancy hand-embroidered tablecloths and any table or bureau scarves or runners had to be ironed in a very special way... always on the wrong side to bring out the needlework.

The generations today have no conception of the labor involved in those days of no washing machines, and it was an exciting day when a brand new Savage washing machine was delivered and hooked to the faucet over the tubs. However, the clothes still had to be put through a bluing rinse and starched separately. As a hangover from those days, I still prefer to hang the laundry on the line for the breezes and sun to do their work, not to mention the exercise!

Peter always seemed to have time to help me with little projects and even built me a play house of several rooms, where I kept house and cooked for my raggedy old dolls. He regretted hanging an old tire from the tall *kiawe* tree when he had to push me so frequently!

I remember so well the day Peter and I decided to build a little fishpond in the middle of one of my mother's flower beds. We had mixed the cement and, of course, I had my hands in the mixture as though I was mixing poi... when the water stopped running! How we ever survived that one is something I've forgotten.

Saturday was the day to turn the house asunder. It was Peter's job to drag out the Chinese rugs and runners, haul them up to the clothesline, then proceed to beat out the dust. He also had to remove the potted plants from the living and dining rooms to replace them later with fresh ferns or flowers, and run the heavy waxer over the 'ohia wood floors once a month.

Then Rachel and Mary cleared the ceilings of cobwebs with a long-handled brush covered with a clean cloth; oiled the furniture, especially the special rosewood chairs made by the artisan, Ah Chong; checked every nook and cranny, polished the floors and tended the maidenhair in the fernery. By the end of the working day, the house smelled of a mixture of furniture polish and damp earth.

One of our fun pastimes was to cool off in the small cement pool in the fernery that had a 'sort of fountain' in the middle that spouted water up to the ceiling, much to my parents' dismay. We would curl ourselves up around the spigot, hang on and gather up speed by going round and round until we were dizzy and most of the water had splashed out. Thankfully, there was a drain in the cement floor and the walls were of lava rock.

After all that cleaning of the living areas of the house, the actual hub of the house was the large, airy kitchen that had a special kind of warmth. There was lots of counter space with cupboards underneath for canned goods and oversized pots and pans where we kids could easily hide when playing hide and seek or sardines. Above the counters were large glassed-in cupboards with shelves that held china and crystal, and a little black safe for the flat silver stood in a corner.

The tin bread box and bins for rice, flour and sugar were on a separate shelf next to open shelves for pots, bowls, casseroles, and all sizes of heavy black iron frying pans. The large Alexander & Baldwin calendar that hung over the bins listed all the ships' arrivals and departures from the West Coast and the Orient, which, of course, was pretty important in those days when ships were our sole life line to the outside world!

The kitchen could easily be turned into a preserve factory, restaurant or bakery. In one corner was a large gas range with six burners, three ovens and a warming oven to keep serving dishes ready. On the ledge above the burners were jars of Hawaiian salt, chili pepper water, soy, Crisco and a glass jar containing all the burned matches.

The original sink was made of zinc until it was replaced with a standard four-legged white tile sink. Even today, many kama'aina refer to that area as "the zinc." All the cleaning products… coconut brushes, link-chain scrubbers, Old Dutch, Sapolio… were kept on an open shelf under the sink, and a big agate dishpan hung on a nail. At the end of the drainboard hung an erstwhile kerosene can for slops, which was picked up every other day and replaced with a clean can.

In the middle of the room was the large zinc-topped kitchen table that was used for snacking, preparing vegetables, mixing cakes and rolling out pastry dough, or even converted to an ironing board for large tablecloths by covering it completely with blankets and a sheet.

But making mango chutney was a project! Peter, who knew how to pick just the right mangoes… not too green and not too ripe… was sent up into the trees. Then everyone was set to the task of peeling and slicing mangoes until our hands were black! Mercifully, the slices were put in large wooden chopping bowls, sprinkled generously with Hawaiian rock salt, covered with dishtowels and left to sit overnight.

The next day the real work began! The trusty, heavy old meat grinder was screwed on to the kitchen table and a large bowl placed beneath to catch the drippings. The grinder was duly fed with peeled and quartered onions which produced a mass crying jag, de-seeded chili peppers, raisins, dried apricots, pieces of scraped and preserved ginger, cloves upon cloves of garlic and boxes of glazed fruit cake mix. The cooking process took hours, but the jarring, the pouring of paraffin and the final sealing took time, too. The jars were subsequently wiped and labeled and stored in cartons in the large cement basement below the kitchen, along with various and sundry discards, old magazines and newspapers, more jars and generations of Charlotte's webs.

Guava jelly-making was a time for cautious treading through the kitchen. Numerous jelly bags holding the stewed fruit hung from broom and mop handles teetering between chairs, counters or whatever space was convenient, and left to drip into bowls overnight. The bottles of clear, light-colored jelly and dark jam were also stored below. *Poha* jam was actually a year-round procedure as the berries grew wild in the backyard.

Fruits of all description were piled high in various baskets on the counters for snacks or quickly consumed in salads, fruit cocktails and soups.

The day the two-door refrigerator with the humming engine sitting right on top arrived to replace the old icebox was an exciting one, indeed! That is, until we were faced with the pesky defrosting process.

However, the gelatin dishes were almost miraculous compared to the times the same dishes teetered on the block of ice in the old icebox.

Maybe the saying "greatest thing since sliced bread" originated in our youth. Loaves of white or brown bread sold for a nickel... unsliced... so the wooden bread board and trusty bread knife had their own special spot near the toaster on a small table with the ever-popular waffle iron. It was a great treat to have rye or raisin bread for a change, and really glamorous to have specially ordered pink loaves of bread for tea party sandwiches.

Entertaining was always done in the home with preferably sit-down dinners that began with a soup or fruit cocktail, a salad with the entrée and a very special dessert. Coffee was served either in the living room or on the lanai.

When my mother had one of her small poi suppers, she considered the flowers, the table arrangements, music and entertainment as much a part of the menu as the *kaukau*. Everything was geared to creating an atmosphere of informal Hawaiian hospitality and aloha.

Ti leaves for the table had to be washed and stripped of the mid rib, then placed on the protecting butcher paper so that the effect was a shiny green tablecloth. We picked plumerias, stuck them on toothpicks and then on to cabbages to make pom-poms for centerpieces; or interspersed lei of the same flowers with delicate ferns around partly sliced watermelon or prepared pineapple… or even just baskets of all kinds of colorful fruit with ti leaf bows. There really wasn't much room for the decor because the various coconut dishes of food fanning out from each place took up a lot of space, too.

Just before the guests arrived, leis were draped on the back of each chair and the musicians, strategically ensconced. The boys were familiar with most of the *kama'aina* guests and always honored them with a song composed especially for them. If they were seated, they had to stand while the song was being played.

Those were the days of prohibition, but my father had a 'friend' who came by night to supply him with aged *'okolehao* in a barrel which was served before dinner. Women were always beautifully groomed in the traditional silk *holoku* with a sweeping train, and the men wore the usual white trousers, white silk shirt and a red silk sash around the waist. The hot food was served piping hot, everyone welcomed seconds of their favorite dish, yet left enough room for the light-as-a-feather coconut cake, with its creamy filling and the frosting sprinkled with the pristinely white flakes of coconut that I had grated on the ancient grater. Besides the cake, there were always dishes of *haupia*, *kulolo* and small pieces of sweet sugar cane.

The usual family dinner consisted of either rice or poi, fish, meat or chicken and a fresh vegetable. Salads were usually fresh Manoa lettuce with sliced tomato and Thousand Island Dressing, our favorite.

At least once or twice a month the family enjoyed tripe stew, tongue, liver and bacon and, as a special treat, homemade laulau and fat, sweet *'ama'ama*, or mullet, wrapped in ti leaves and steamed in the oven.

It was always a lark to go shopping with my mother at the old fish market on Kekaulike Street, where the Chinese hawkers stood over their freshest fish imbedded in chipped ice, bloody carcasses of meat or under plucked chickens hanging by the neck. Marketing was a great time for our elders to visit with friends, and between them they could pretty much control the price of fish with their collective bargaining powers. The men still made a profit, though. Everything was wrapped in ti leaves and old newspaper.

But it was the Hawaiian booths that intrigued me the most… it was more like going into someone's kitchen compared to the white-tiled icy stalls of the old hawkers with their bloody aprons and waterlogged hands.

The glassed-in case displayed oily balls of *inamona*, various kinds of *limu*, jars of red salt, and packages of coarser white rock salt, old Worcestershire bottles of chili pepper water, jars of dried fish and bowls of prepared raw fish and crabs. Behind the case stood a small oilcloth-covered table with mugs, a can of Carnation milk and a bowl of sugar, pots of steaming laulau, bundles of stacked ti leaves and a large barrel of poi. The family members happily exchanged the latest gossip while dispensing the food and scooping up thick poi into cotton bags that sold for a quarter, 50 cents or a dollar.

My mother had her favorite *limu* for certain dishes and there was always an ample supply of *limu* jars in the icebox. Long strands of green *limu-'ele'ele* was a must for stew, and raw fish wasn't good unless it was *lomi*-ed with *limu-kohu*.

Summers were spent living in country houses on the beach at Punalu'u. TV was unheard of, but kids in those days never lacked for amusement and the days never seemed long enough! With the lapping waves right at our doorstep, we spent hours in the water swimming out to a raft, or preferably an anchored sampan, to haul ourselves up and either dive or jump, playing "King of the Castle." We waded around, peering down at sea life through a glass box, always leery of the lurking eels. We gathered buckets of sand crabs at night just for the sport, but set crab nets by day… the smellier the bait, the better.

We hiked up into the valleys to pick yellow ginger buds just before they really opened for our leis, gorged on mountain apples, gathered guavas for jelly and stalked *'opae* in the river; we risked our necks bodysurfing at Pounders in La'ie; watched the fishermen lay the *hukilau* nets at night and were right there the next morning to help haul them in; we rode coconut leaves tied to the back of a car that towed us around expansive lawns, and made fudge all hours of the day or night.

The Hawaiian family who had lived down the beach for generations was having a lu'au to celebrate the completion of their new house, and we were more than welcome to join in with the gang that was gathering to help. It was definitely a family affair, with relatives arriving from Kaua'i bearing red Hawaiian salt and purple poi, and others from Maui with sweet onions and seafood. Soon there were squid and slit fish hanging up to dry on the clothesline.

A few days before the party, one of the granddaughters and I helped her mother and *tutu* gather *limu-kohu* along the reef but slipped away when they began cleaning the *'opala* from delicate strands while gossiping in Hawaiian.

We thought it would be much more daring to join the *'opihi* pickers as they flattened themselves against the rocks to face the crashing waves until the water receded then quickly turned to pry the stubborn limpets off the rocks before the next wave. But, on second thought, we settled on chasing black crabs and collecting *pipipi* along the rocks.

Everyone joined in for the *hukilau*. Thrashing the water with ti leaves and pulling in nets full of wriggling fish was great sport! Then we tagged along with the kids going up in the mountains in search of wild fruit, ginger and *maile* for leis, ferns for table decoration and the edible kind. We weren't considered agile enough to shimmy up the coconut trees for nuts!

The morning of the party we helped the young girls cover the boards laid on wooden saw-horses with butcher paper, then laid ti leaves close together for the tablecloth, and watched a gray-haired lady decorate the table with lacy ferns, clusters of fresh fruit and flowers... all from simple offerings from the mountains and backyards.

Finally the party began, everyone knew one another, 'okolehao flowed, there were lots of lei and kissing and everyone was in a happy party mood. *Tutu* took the occasion to show off her heirloom *holoku* made of rich brocade from China, and was treated like royalty as she sat fanning herself and sipping 'okolehao.

When Grandpa called, we all gathered round the pit in the backyard to watch the pig being brought out of the *imu*, then scurried towards the tables to begin the feast! We kids were impatient for Grandpa to finish saying the blessing so we could reach for the bottles of orange, cream, root beer and strawberry soda water lined up on the table.

Later after the lively music and dancing was *pau*, people finally went home with their *puolo* of food. It had been an exciting few days for us kids, and we had also learned a lot from these hospitable country people.

During the summer we got to visit with our 'ohana who lived at nearby Kahuku plantation. Whenever we spent the night with them, we were awakened by the five o'clock whistle that summoned all the workers, but slept until the man of the house returned on his break to eat a hearty breakfast. We loved playing with plantation kids whose families were always so hospitable. The plantation carpenter's wife welcomed us with, "Eat, eat!" as she placed dishes of sashimi, sushi or sukiyaki in front of us. We learned how to use chopsticks eating family style in the kitchen and began our life-long appreciation of hot, spicy Korean foods. We gorged on Manuel's mother's crusty, doughy loaves of bread that she baked in outside ovens, but much preferred our dry fish to their *bacalhao*. We still fall back on a recipe that comes nearest to Manuel's mother's real Portuguese bean soup!

The most fun we had at night was when we all went to the movies at the Kahuku theatre and were especially rowdy brats when the projector broke down or rats ran among the aisles.

We hated to see the end of summer! Sleeping under the stars; discovering all the wild fruits abounding in the valleys with their different smells and tastes of the Islands; learning to strum an ukulele; the muddy taro patches; the smell of *ehu kai* and the sound of pounding surf rounding the bend of the bay; the abundance of fresh fish; the happy people with their, "*Mai, mai, hele mai ai*. Plenty *kaukau!*"... the truly original Hawaiian hospitality! The way of life in Hawai'i was unique, and we took it all for granted.

It's all been a great influence on my life... all memories we can now share.

Hawaiian Garden

When you think of the Hawaiian Islands, what flora comes quickly to mind? Pineapple, guava, papaya, mangoes… all and more that make up an exotic picture of riotous colors, interesting textures and tantalizing tastes!

The names of the early pioneers who transplanted and cultivated the native plants we know and enjoy today may have been forgotten, but by their foresight Hawai'i has been blessed with the ingredients for a fabulous tropical garden.

So let's pick a sunny day to amble through a typical Hawaiian garden filled with plants of all description nurtured for beauty, smell, nutrition and nostalgia!

A… An *awai* to run through the garden for music, *'opae* darting and hiding 'neath the rocks, and where watercress may thrive.

B… Bananas with all that potassium, raw, baked or fried and baked in breads and cakes.

C… Citrus, all kinds of oranges, limes and lemons, especially delicious when their blossoms fill the air with their pungent aroma, and the carambola tree with its golden star fruit.

D… Durian tree, just to remind us that King Kalakaua sent it back from Asia while traveling around the world, and forgive him its *pilau* smell because the fruit is so delicious.

E… *'Elepaio* birds must abound to dart in and out of the trees and feast on the pesky aphids.

F… Fig trees to wrap in netting to preserve the luscious fruit to enjoy with thick cream.

G… Guavas for juice and preserves full of vitamin C, and maybe some grapes to cover an arbor as in the past.

H… Hawaiian chili peppers, the hottest thing in any garden, but such an important item in many a dish.

I… *Ilima* bushes of delicate golden blossoms to remind us of our ali'i.

J… Java plum trees, messy maybe, but a staunch windbreak for other planting and their tart, purple fruit the birds love.

1

K... *Kukui* trees for their distinctive green color and the nuts with all their many uses.

L... *Lilikoi* vines growing wild in one corner for lots of juice, and *laukahi*, my favorite Hawaiian herb with all its medicinal value.

M... Mango trees towering above our garden laden with fruit for feasting while hanging over the sink and for the many jars of chutney to share with friends.

N... None, noted for its medicinal properties even in this modern world.

O... *'Ohi'a-'ai*, as the Hawaiians called the luscious mountain apple, and, of course, a true *'ohia* tree for is wispy red *lehua* blossoms to attract the bees.

P... Papayas for our daily breakfast fruit, *Poha* for our favorite jam and *palapalai* fern thriving in a cool spot for hat lei.

Q... Quince, the flowering variety, to cut and bring in the house to herald spring.

R... Rose Apple for its delicate flavored fruit.

S... Soursop for luscious mousses, and sugar cane, just a small clump somewhere like all *kama'aina* gardens used to have.

T... Taro and ti, the mainstays of the Hawaiians.

U... *Ulu*, the breadfruit tree with its delicious golden fruit to cook and enjoy slathered in butter!

V... Violets! Every garden needs a border of little purple and white blossoms hidden among the rich green leaves to hunt and pick, and a Violet tree to give them shade.

W... Wi tree towering above all else with its prickly-centered fruit you so seldom see today.

X... to mark the spot for rest and contemplation in the garden.

Y... Yesterday, today, tomorrow bushes with their white, lavender and purple flowers ever changing.

Z... Zinnias, beds of multicolored flowers to remind us of the old mama-sans peddling their baskets of flowers wrapped in newspaper and chanting, "Frawah, frawah foah only one quatah."

Oh, what a happy retreat of memories and beauty this garden would be!!!

Definitions of Foods

Since Hawai'i has earned the sobriquet of the "Melting Pot of the Pacific," and all the different ethnic groups use so many Island products and have also introduced many new ones from their lands, let's look at some of the words we may take for granted but which may be Greek to the next fella! Many a delicious dish has been passed up from sheer ignorance of what it was.

Aburage: Fried bean curd sold cut in brown triangular pieces about 3/4 inch thick. It's used mainly in the making of cone sushi, but can be sliced and used in a variety of Japanese dishes.

Adobo: Popular Filipino entrée of seasoned meat or a combination of pork and chicken.

Bagoong: Filipino fish sauce made from a mixture of salt, small fish like anchovies, shrimps, clams or oysters, and fermented to a sauce or paste. Used in flavoring dishes.

Burdock: *Gobo*, a long, thin root found in the vegetable section of the market and used mostly in Japanese cooking.

Camote: Filipino name for the leaves of the sweet potato vine.

Carne de Vinha D'Alhos: Favorite Portuguese dish of very peppery pickled pork (usually sliced but can be whole) marinated for several days in chili pepper, garlic and vinegar, then fried or baked. It is an old Portuguese custom to serve this dish on Christmas morning.

Char Siu: Chinese sweet roast pork, soaked in red coloring and roasted. It has a strong anise flavor, and is a familiar sight hanging over the meat stalls in Chinatown markets.

Chow Fun: A popular Chinese dish of wide noodles, meat and vegetable.

Chook: Another favorite Chinese soup of turkey bones, ginger, rice and seasonings cooked in stock until it reaches a gruel consistency. Served with Chinese parsley.

Daikon: Japanese name for turnip or white radish.

Dasheen: Japanese variety of taro.

Dim Sum: Chinese steamed dumplings filled with a variety of meat, seafood and vegetables. Usually a variety of dim sum is offered from a trolley in Chinese restaurants.

Goa: Wing beans; popular in Filipino dishes cooked with meat and other vegetables or in soups.

Gobo: Burdock, a root.

Haha: Stalk of the taro plant, peeled, chopped and cooked until quite soft and served as a green vegetable with lots of butter and salt and pepper.

He'e: Octopus or squid; speared usually by fishermen.

I'a-ota: Tahitian raw fish made with lime juice and coconut cream.

Inamona: Hawaiian relish of roasted *kukui* nuts pounded to a paste.

Kalua pig: The whole pig steamed in an underground oven (*imu*) for several hours; the star attraction at a lu'au.

Kamaboko: Japanese fish cake sold on boards or in rounds in the fish/meat department of markets.

Kanten: Japanese gelatin like agar-agar used in making desserts.

Kau Yuk: Red pot roast pork; Chinese dish of fresh belly pork steamed with seasonings and served with thin steamed buns.

Kim Chee: Highly seasoned Korean relish using mainly *won bok* cabbage and chili pepper.

Ko'elepalau: Hawaiian pudding made of sweet potato and coconut.

Kulolo: Hawaiian dessert of taro and coconut steamed in ti or banana leaves.

Laulau: A bundle of pork, taro leaves, sometimes salt salmon or butter fish, wrapped in ribbed ti leaves and steamed for 4 hours. Sometimes chicken is substituted for the pork.

Lawalu Fish: Fresh Island fish wrapped in cleaned and ribbed ti leaves securely fastened and steamed or baked in the oven or *imu*.

Long Rice: An Oriental pasta; a translucent pasta or bean thread pressed from mungo beans. Used mostly in combination with chicken in a soup-based dish.

Lumpia: Filipinos use this as a wrapper when rolling up fillings of meat or seafood and vegetables and deep fried.

Lup Cheong: Chinese smoked pork sausage. Delicious steamed over a pot of cooking rice.

Maki Sushi: Rice seasoned with sweet vinegar sauce, layered with vegetables and fish and rolled in black seaweed.

Malasadas: Popular Portuguese sweet doughnuts made with yeast and deep fried.

Mann Doo: Dumplings of won ton pi folded around a mixture of pork and vegetables and dropped in boiling water or soup.

Miso: Fermented rice and soy bean paste. Popular in soups and as a seasoning. Sold in cartons in the market.

Mochi: Japanese New Year custom to pound glutinous rice for these special rice cakes.

Mungo Beans: Dried green beans used in cooking or soaked in water to make bean sprouts to use in salads.

Mochiko: Flour made from glutinous rice.

Mirin: Sweet Japanese vinegar used in cooking and a popular salad dressing for dieters.

Namasu: Japanese salad made of cucumber, carrots or daikon mixed in flavored vinegar.

Nishime: Popular Japanese dish made with various vegetables, seaweed and dasheen. More flavorful cooked with meat.

'Opae: Small fresh water shrimp found in cool, shady mountain streams, usually under black rocks.

'Okolehao: Potent liquor made from the root of ti plant and fermented.

'Opihi: Hawaiian limpet found on wave-swept rocks. Meat is removed from shells and eaten raw. Due to scarcity and the dangers in gathering 'opihi, the price has skyrocketed today so that it is considered quite a delicacy and served sparingly at a lu'au.

Pansit: Filipino dish of noodles, meat and vegetables, usually a combination of chicken, pork and shrimp.

Pao Doce: Portuguese sweet bread. On special occasions it is baked with hard boiled eggs, a ring and various trinkets. Another "must" served on Christmas morning in accordance with Portuguese custom.

Patis: Filipino fish sauce used in seasoning, drained off the fermented seafood, *bagoong*.

Pepeau: Dry fungus found on rotting *hau* trees, similar to mushrooms but crunchy and flavorful.

Pipi: Small black mollusk found along the rocky shoreline.

Pipikaula: Hawaiian version of dried beef jerky. Strips of salted meat are usually dried in screened boxes left in the sunshine.

Poi: Hawaiian staff of life; cooked taro pounded and thinned with water to one- or two-finger consistency.

Pulehu: Hawaiian method of broiling fish or meat over charcoal.

Puolo: a holder for lei or food wrapped in ti leaves and securely fastened; usually given as a token to take home leftovers at a luau.

Sake: Japanese rice wine.

Sashimi: sliced raw fish served on a bed of shredded lettuce, cabbage, daikon or carrots with a hot mustard/soy sauce. Originally only on the Japanese menus but now a universal favorite *pupu* in the Islands with several new versions.

Senbei: Variety of crispy cookies made with rice and wheat flour. Fortune cookies are one of the more popular.

Sesame Seed Oil: Used sparingly in Oriental cooking for frying or seasoning.

Shibi: Tuna.

Somen: Very fine noodles. Excellent in salads.

Stir Fry: Oriental style of quick frying meats and vegetables over high heat. Usually cooked in an Oriental wok.

Sukiyaki: Japanese meal cooked in skillets or in pans over small hibachis (iron container of burning coals). Meat is stir-fried, seasoned with soy and sake and combined with chopped vegetables. Served as the piéce de résistance in a Japanese Tea House.

Tako: Japanese translation for octopus.

Takuan: Oriental pickled daikon.

Tempura: Seafoods or vegetables dipped in fritter batter and deep fried.

Teriyaki: Japanese marinade sauce made from soy, sugar, fresh ginger and garlic. Used for marinating meat or chicken.

Ti: The green leaf used in cooking. Root of the plant made potent drink, *ʻokolehao*.

Tofu: Soybean curd pressed into cubes and packaged in cartons of water. Usually found in the vegetable section of the markets.

Wana: Sea urchin with spines… avoid these in the ocean and on the reef. The orange tongues inside the shells are considered a delicacy by the Hawaiians when properly prepared.

Wok: Shallow round bottom pan used in Oriental cooking.

Wun Tun: Triangles made by stuffing the wrapper (*won ton pi*) with pork or shrimp mixture and cooking them in deep fat until crispy and golden. Usually served with a mustard/soy sauce. Excellent *pupu*.

Won Ton Pi: Chinese doily made of dough that is sold in three-inch-square packets in the refrigerator section of the markets.

Avocado

My love for avocados began many years ago, only back then we didn't call them by that name, we called them alligator pears and devoured them avidly just plain or with catsup, soy or lemon juice and even just a sprinkling of sugar! Dinner usually included an avocado cocktail or little balls of the rich fruit floating in a clear consommé. We enjoyed every mouthful even though we knew they were fattening! The smooth, creamy, buttery fruit was like no other Island delight.

Our kitchen counters seemed to always be littered with green and brown alligator pears of all shapes and sizes. There was always lots to share with friends and enough to be left to ripen for four or five days. If my mother was having one of her ladies' luncheons and needed 'those calories' in a hurry, they were, stored in a brown paper bag to ripen until fully soft and ready to eat. Then they were popped in the refrigerator. One of my favorite pastimes was sticking a toothpick in the *puka* where the stem had been to see if they were ripe.

Another childhood memory was coveting the discarded seed and propping it up with three toothpicks in a glass jar half filled with water. It was a lesson in patience to play the waiting game for two to six weeks to see the seed crack open and the hairy roots start descending into the water and a fragile, leafy stalk emerge to the light.

After that, the excitement was lost and propagating forgotten.

Historically, avocados go back quite a long ways. In 1519 Hernando Cortez, a Spanish soldier of fortune, landed in Mexico City and discovered the most versatile fruit of the New World… the avocado! In 1526, Oviedo, a historian, wrote of the avocado: "In the center of the fruit is a seed like a Peeled chestnut, and between this and the rind is an abundant part which is eaten… a paste similar to butter and a very good taste."

The English named it avocado, the Spanish abogado, and the French called it avocat… probably all derived from attempting to pronounce the Aztec name, ahuacatl.

Don Francisco de Paula Marin, a Spanish horticulturist renowned for his importation of many Island fruits, is credited with having planted the first avocado trees in Hawai'i before 1825, and by 1855 the fruit was thriving throughout the Islands. In 1895 Admiral Beardslee introduced Guatamalan seedlings and since then agriculturists have been experimenting and improving the texture and flavor of the Islands' year-round crops.

Avocados are usually available at both supermarkets and farmers' markets.

Avocado is so high in fat content that half of a winter avocado provides about 247 calories, but the oil makes it one of our most digestible foods. It also has a very high potassium content.

Once fully ripe, soft and ready to eat, avocados should be refrigerated until needed, but not for long, as they tend to turn color and become softer.

Never freeze avocados whole, only after they have been puréed.

To prevent the fruit from darkening, brush the cut surface with lemon juice.

When storing a half of an avocado, replace the seed, brush with lemon, wrap in saran then refrigerate.

To save time before tossing avocados into a salad, peel the fruit, slice carefully around the seed, lather it with lemon juice, wrap in saran and refrigerate. When ready to use, simply lift the slices off the seed gently with a knife.

For half shells: halve avocados lengthwise, twist gently to separate halves, and whack a sharp knife directly into the seed and twist to lift out. Use half shells with or without skins.

For rings: halve avocado crosswise, whack out seed and peel, then slice across.

For slices: place peeled halves cut-side down to prevent browning. Cut lengthwise or crosswise into crescents. Lengthwise slices may be diced or cut into cubes.

For purée: mash peeled avocado with fork, force through a sieve or purée in electric mixer and blend with some lemon juice.

Avocados go a long way. They can comprise a full luncheon or light supper and serve as *pupu*, soup, salad, dessert, or just as a garnish.

Avocado combines well with vinegar and acid fruits.

Chicken, crab, lobster, shrimp and tuna salads are all tasty when served stuffed in avocado halves. Or place a helping of salad on crisp lettuce leaves or chopped watercress and garnish with slices of avocado and tomato wedges for color.

For a sandwich spread: mash the pulp and combine with catsup, mayonnaise, lemon juice or vinegar and grated onion to spreading consistency. Add cubes or balls of avocados to soups and consommés as garnish just before serving.

Avocado purée freezes well when blended with sugar and lemon juice. Not so with whole or sliced avocado, as they lose their flavor and become soft and discolored.

Baked avocados are a meal in themselves. Halve as many avocados as persons to be served, remove seeds and, if the opening is too small, scoop out a little of the flesh. Fill the cavities with your favorite creamed fish, well seasoned shrimp, crab, lobster or tuna and sprinkle grated cheddar cheese lightly over the top. Bake about 15 minutes in 350° oven to heat through and melt the cheese.

BASIC GUACAMOLE

2 soft avocados, mashed or puréed
3/4 teaspoon salt

1 tablespoon lemon juice
1/4 teaspoon Worcestershire

Blend all ingredients together and serve with fresh vegetables or corn chips or crackers.

Variations on Guacamole.

Add: 2 medium tomatoes, diced
1/2 c green onions, sliced
1/2 lb. bacon, cooked and crumbled
1/2 c sour cream
1/2 c green chiles, diced

1-3/8 oz. envelope onion soup mix
Tabasco sauce to taste
1 c yogurt
2 tablespoons chives

AVOCADO SPREAD

Combine 4 avocados, mashed or puréed, one (1-3/8 ounce) envelope onion soup mix, 2 tablespoons lemon juice and 1/2 cup sour cream. Mix well, cover and chill. Makes about 3-1/2 cups.

DICED AVOCADO COCKTAIL

Diced avocado makes a tasty cocktail to serve as a dinner beginner. Combine 1/2 cup each table cream and tomato paste with 1 teaspoon each salt, Worcestershire and minced celery, 1 tablespoon vinegar and dash of pepper. Chill thoroughly and serve over diced avocado.

AVOCADO SPINACH SOUP

2 avocados
1 package 10 oz. frozen spinach,
   cooked and drained well
1-1/4 c chicken broth or bouillon
1 c heavy cream

1/2 teaspoon each salt and onion salt
dash of white pepper
1/4 teaspoon lemon peel, grated
3 tablespoons lemon juice

Purée avocados with spinach and blend with remaining ingredients; cover and chill thoroughly. Garnish with lemon slices and sieved hard-cooked egg. 6 to 8 servings.

AVOCADO SOUP WITH WATERCRESS

2 avocados, halved and peeled
2 c watercress sprigs
1-1/2 c chicken broth or bouillon
1 c heavy cream

3/4 teaspoon salt
1/8 teaspoon onion salt
2 t lemon juice

Purée avocados with cress and broth and blend until cress is finely chopped. Mix with remaining ingredients and chill thoroughly. 6 to 8 servings

Avocado and Pomelo or Grapefruit Salad

3 avocados, diced   Bib lettuce
3 c pomelo sections, broken up   Watercress

Chop lettuce or watercress into a large bowl, mix in the pomelo and blend in your favorite spicy French dressing. Add the diced avocado and toss gently with more dressing if needed. Serve cold.

Molded Avocado Ring

2 tablespoons gelatin   1 tablespoon onion, grated
1/2 c cold water   2-1/4 teaspoon salt
1-1/4 c hot water   2 drops Tabasco sauce
4 tablespoons lemon juice   3 c avocado, sieved
3/4 c celery, chopped   3/4 c mayonnaise

Sprinkle gelatin over cold water. When mixture has thickened, dissolve in hot water. Add remaining ingredients and pour into oiled 8-inch ring mold. Chill in refrigerator. Unmold on lettuce and fill center with your favorite seafood, chicken or citrus fruit salad. 8-10 servings.

Baked Stuffed Avocado

3 avocados   dash of salt, pepper and cayenne
1/4 c lime juice   2 tablespoons green pepper, chopped
2 c crab meat, flaked or chicken, chopped 1 teaspoon onion, minced
1 c cream sauce   1 c cheese, grated

Cut avocados in half lengthwise, remove pits, sprinkle with lemon juice and salt. Combine seafood or chicken with cream sauce, season to taste and fill avocados with mixture. Sprinkle with grated cheese. Arrange avocados in a baking pan with 1/2 inch of water in the bottom. Bake in a 350° oven for 15 minutes or until cheese melts and sauce is heated through.

Avocado Crepes With Shrimp

Crepes: Add 4 eggs, 1/2 cup flour, 1/4 teaspoon salt, 1/2 cup milk and 1 to 2 tablespoons water to 1/2 cup mashed avocado. With a whisk, blend mixture until smooth. Griddles up about 10 to 12 crepes.

Filling: Melt 2 tablespoons butter and stir in 3 tablespoons flour. Gradually add 1-1/2 cups heated milk and stir constantly until sauce begins to thicken. Add 2 ounces diced Swiss cheese and cook until melted. Remove from heat and stir in 1/2 teaspoon Worcestershire sauce, salt and pepper to taste and 1 pound cleaned shrimp.

Place portion of the filling on each crepe and fold, arrange in single layer in a well-greased baking dish, sprinkle with 3 ounces grated Swiss cheese and dot with 1/4 cup butter. Bake in 400° oven for 10 to 15 minutes until hot and cheese is melted. Serve immediately.

These crepes may be prepared in advance and frozen before baking. Wrap dish in freezer foil and freeze. Bake, wrapped in foil, in hot oven, 400°, for 15 minutes. Remove foil and bake uncovered 15 minutes longer.

Avocado Bread

1/2 c avocado, mashed
1/2 c buttermilk
1 egg
1/2 c vegetable oil
2 c all purpose flour

3/4 c sugar
1/2 teaspoon baking soda
1/2 teaspoon baking powder
1/4 teaspoon salt
3/4 c pecans, chopped

In a medium bowl, mix avocado, egg, buttermilk and oil until blended. Add flour mixed with sugar, baking soda, baking powder, salt and pecans. Mix only until blended, do not overmix. Pour batter into a 9x5-inch greased loaf pan and bake in 350° oven for 55 minutes to 1 hour, until toothpick inserted in center comes out clean. Cool 10 minutes and turn out of pan, slice and serve warm with butter.

Avocado and Chicken Salad

3 c cooked chicken, diced
1-1/2 c celery, diced
4 hard cooked eggs, diced
1/2 c toasted almonds, slivered
1/2 c pineapple bits

1/2 c Miracle Whip salad dressing
1 tablespoon juice from pineapple
3 avocados, peeled, seeded and halved
lettuce leaves for garnish

Mix chicken, celery, eggs, almonds and pineapple with Miracle Whip which has been thinned with pineapple juice. Heap mixture into avocado halves on lettuce leaves. Serve cold. 6 servings.

Sloppy Joes

Pam Spray
1 c onions, chopped
2 lbs. ground beef
4 8-oz. cans tomato sauce
2/3 c green pepper, chopped

1 teaspoon salt
dash of pepper
3 avocados, thinly sliced
8 hamburger buns, split, toasted
    and buttered

Sauté onions and beef in sprayed pan until browned. Add tomato sauce, green pepper and seasonings and cook until bubbly. Spoon beef mixture over buns and top with avocado slices. 8 generous servings.

Avocado Soufflé

2 avocados, puréed with 1/4 c lime juice
1 envelope unflavored gelatin
3/4 c sugar
1/8 teaspoon salt

4 eggs, separated
1/4 c water
3 tablespoons light rum
1 c heavy cream, whipped

Combine gelatin, 1/4 cup sugar and salt in top of double boiler. Beat egg yolks with water and add to gelatin. Stir over boiling water until gelatin is dissolved, about 5 minutes. Remove from heat, stir in rum and avocado puree. Cool until mixture mounds slightly when dropped from a spoon.

Beat egg whites until foamy; gradually beat in remaining sugar until stiff, but not dry. Fold with whipped cream into gelatin mixture. Pour into a 1-quart soufflé dish and chill until firm. Serve with 1/2 cup heavy cream mixed with 1 tablespoon light rum.

Avocado Cheese Cake

Set aside 1 prepared
    graham cracker crust
1 avocado, seeded and peeled
1 8-oz. package cream cheese

1/2 c sour cream
3 to 4 lemon strips
1 3-3/4 oz. package vanilla
    instant pudding pie filling

Blend first four ingredients until smooth, set aside. Make pudding mix according to directions and combine with other ingredients, blend until mixed well. Pour into crust and chill. 6 servings.

Avocado Lime Pie

1 avocado puréed with
    1/2 cup fresh lemon juice
1 c sugar
1 envelope unflavored gelatin
1/4 teaspoon salt

3 eggs, separated
1/2 c milk
1 tablespoon lime peel, grated
9-inch baked pie shell
Sweetened whipped cream for garnish

In top of double boiler, combine: 1/2 cup sugar, gelatin and salt. Beat egg yolks lightly with milk and stir in. Stir over boiling water until gelatin dissolves, about 5 minutes. Remove from heat; stir in lime peel, then avocado purée and chill until mixture mounds slightly when dropped from spoon. Beat egg whites gradually with remaining 1/2 cup sugar, until stiff, but not dry. Fold into avocado mixture and turn into pie shell. Chill until firm and garnish with whipped cream.

Avocado Cream

1 ripe avocado (to equal 8 oz.
    when peeled and pitted)
juice of half a lime or lemon

3 teaspoons superfine sugar
1/2 c heavy whipping cream

Peel the avocado, remove pit, cut into cubes and process until smooth. Add the sugar, lime or lemon juice and cream and blend thoroughly. Pour into serving cups, chill for at least an hour and serve. 2-to 4-persons servings.

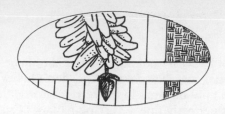

Banana

In the days of large homes, sprawling lawns, towering trees, adequate gardeners and indoor help, most *kama'aina* vegetable gardens had a patch of apple or Bluefield bananas that were cut down when the fruit was still green but mature. The stalks of bananas, still dripping with juice that stained badly, were tied securely with rope and then hung to ripen from a sturdy hook placed above the railing of the back porch, a central thoroughfare to the large kitchen.

The screen door swung open to let in the slop man to exchange clean buckets for buckets of discarded food for his pigs; the iceman with his 50-pound block of ice for the special compartment of the old icebox; the milkman with his bottles of rich milk topped with inches of thick cream that had to be 'cut' before pouring, and yardmen leaving buckets of citrus and other fruits, vegetables and cut flowers.

Bananas, one of the essential food plants the early Polynesians brought with them to their new home in Hawai'i, are still an important food of the daily diet in Hawai'i. Bananas were restricted to chiefs and priests to be eaten at ceremonial feasts. Women were forbidden all but two varieties, and were still forbidden the fruit when Captain Cook discovered the Hawaiian Islands in 1778 and found the fruit thriving. In ancient times there were 70 or more varieties known to the natives, of which only 20 or 30 varieties of ornamental and eating bananas are known today.

Mai'a, the Hawaiian name for banana, is referred to as the 'tree of birth and life' or 'life out of death.' You can never kill a banana plant. As the fruit destroys the tree, new plants spring up from the old stumps. Once the green bananas are picked, the tree should be cut down so that shoots or suckers soon begin to grow up around the base of the old plant.

Bananas know no season, and are one of the most popular fruits grown in the Islands. They can be used in soups, salads, entrées, baked goods and desserts and fried or baked for a starch.

There are several different varieties of delicious eating bananas: the Cavendish group consisting of Chinese, Williams, Valery and Hamakua. There are the regular Bluefields and the Dwarf Bluefields. The Brazilian is mistakenly called Apple in Hawai'i and there is also a Dwarf Brazilian.

Among the most popular varieties of cooking bananas or plantains are Maiamaoli, Popoulu, Iholena, Red and Ice Cream.

To hasten the ripening process, place the bunch in a brown bag and leave in a dark spot. They are best eaten when the fruit is a solid yellow with brown flecks. Cooking bananas should never be eaten raw, but eating bananas may be cooked. And don't believe the old wives' tale that you can't put bananas in the refrigerator… they may discolor but the inside is perfectly fine. Overripe bananas can go directly into the freezer in ziplock bags and used later for baked goods or slushes. Just run frozen banana under warm water, peel with a sharp knife and slice or mash the fruit for puree.

Healthwise, a banana a day is highly recommended for its high supply of potassium. Fully digestible, the fruit is a boon to the elderly and young alike, and babies in Hawai'i are given well mashed or sieved bananas at an early age.

The custom of using sections of the sheaf of the leaf to hold leis and keep them fresh was begun in olden times and is still used today. The natives also fitted one section into another to use as temporary pipes to run water from streams to the house or taro patches. The leaves are still used for cooking and as plates but not for braiding hats. Individual pieces of the trunk make ideal protection for young seedling, especially shade for young lettuce plants. Chunks of the trunk make sturdy bases for floral arrangements.

There are a variety of ways to enjoy bananas.

Boiled Bananas

Place whole unpeeled bananas in boiling water for about 15 minutes, until the peel is transparent in color. Slit the banana lengthwise and serve plain with butter and brown sugar.

Baked Bananas

Place unpeeled bananas on aluminum foil to catch the sticky drippings in a pan with a little water and bake them in a 350° oven for 30 to 40 minutes, or until they pop open. Remove from the oven, slit skin lengthwise and season with butter or oleo, or salt and pepper. Keeping the skins on when serving helps retain the heat and also holds the melting butter.

Bananas En Casserole

Peel bananas and place in a casserole. Dot with butter or margarine and add brown sugar and fruit juice such as lime, lemon, orange, guava or passion fruit juice and bake for 30 minutes or until done. Optional: top with grated coconut.

SAUTÉED BANANAS

Peel ripe bananas and cook the fruit slowly in a frying pan with quite a bit of butter or oleo over medium heat until they are golden brown. Keep turning to make them brown evenly. (Sorry, a spray doesn't work in this process.) Serve as is, or add guava jelly and lemon juice or sherry and baste bananas until they are glazed.

Serve hot with a meat dish, or they're exceptionally good with curry.

Or douse the warm bananas with rum and top with cream for dessert.

BROILED BANANAS

Peel bananas, cut lengthwise and place in a shallow baking dish. Dot with butter or oleo; add guava jelly and lemon juice and place under broiler and baste until bananas are tender and glazed.

BANANA SANDWICH SPREAD

Combine mashed bananas, a squirt of lemon juice and chunky peanut butter. Spread slices of bread with a thin coating of mayonnaise before spreading the mixture.

SIMPLE BANANA SALAD

Peel and scrape off ripe bananas, cut in half lengthwise and lay on a bed of Manoa lettuce. Top with a dollop of mayonnaise, add a cherry for appeal and chopped nuts for crunch.

FRIED BANANAS

Roll bananas in curry powder before frying them slowly in lots of butter until they turn golden brown and are done.

HONEY BAKED BANANAS

Use any variety of bananas. Peel and place whole bananas in a shallow buttered baking dish, as many layers as the dish will hold. Pour honey over all, sprinkle generously with chopped macadamia nuts and squeeze orange juice over all before or after baking. Bake in 350° oven for 1 hour. Serve hot, warm or cold, with or without fresh cream or ice cream.

BAKED BANANAS

Peel and halve 4 bananas in a baking dish, dot with butter and sprinkle over the top allspice, salt and 4 tablespoons guava jelly. Drizzle 1/3 cup white wine over all and bake in 375° oven for 15 minutes.

BAKED BANANAS AU RUM

Make a syrup of 1/2 cup sugar, 1/4 cup lemon juice, 1/2 T butter, 2 tablespoons white rum and simmer for 10 minutes. Peel 6 medium, underripe bananas, slice in half lengthwise and place in a buttered baking dish, cut-side down. Pour syrup over and bake for 30 minutes in 400° oven. Turn once after 15 minutes.

Banana Nut Ring or Bread

This is different and freezes well.

Beat together one (3 ounce) package cream cheese and 1 cup sugar until well blended. Add 1 egg and 1 teaspoon vanilla. Stir in 1-1/2 cups mashed bananas and 1/2 cup chopped pecans.

Sift together 1-1/4 cups flour, 3/4 cup cornmeal, 1 teaspoon each baking powder and soda, 1/2 teaspoon each salt, cinnamon, and 1/2 tablespoon nutmeg. Add to creamed mixture and blend well.

Pour into a well-greased ring mold or loaf pan. Bake for 30 to 35 minutes, or until toothpick comes out clean. Cool in pan 10 minutes then turn out on rack.

Banana Brown Betty

2 c bread crumbs
1 c sugar
2 tablespoon butter
6 large bananas, mashed

Butter baking dish and set oven at 350°.

Mix sugar and crumbs and line a baking dish generously. Pour bananas over evenly and cover with the rest of the bread crumb mixture. Bake 30 minutes.

Breadfruit

Breadfruit was a staple food in the diet of the early Polynesians and prized in many of the Pacific Islands, especially Tahiti and Samoa. The sprouts that grow from the roots of the tree were probably carried as precious cargo to Hawai'i with enough moisture to support their growth.

It's sad that this exceptionally handsome tree, with its pleasing shape and luxuriant, lobe-shaped leathery leaves, that grows to a height of 30 to 60 feet is not planted in more gardens. It has become a symbol of the lush foliage of the tropics in many areas. In the olden days the leaves of the tree were used as sandpaper to smooth and polish coconut bowls and *kukui* nuts. Besides its beauty, the tree is also a great source of food.

The bold design of the breadfruit leaf and its globular fruit was the inspiration for a number of patterns for Hawaiian quilts which have been popular for more than a century. Then in more modern times the breadfruit's decorative pattern has been copied in textiles, jewelry, wooden and glassware and even carvings on furniture.

The fruit, which can weigh up to 10 pounds, has a warty rind and is still immature when pea green. It turns a yellow-green when mature and should be picked, otherwise it softens, falls and bursts into a rotting mess on the ground. Breadfruit can be stored on the counter until it is soft to the touch and ready to cook. To hasten ripening the breadfruit, take out the stem and fill the cavity with salt. In about two days it will be ripe.

In the olden days birds that were valued for their plumage in the making of feather cloaks and lei were snared with the sticky breadfruit gum. This milky sap that exudes all over the fruit when picked was also used as glue or caulking material for canoes. Children coveted it as wads of gum.

At one point in Hawaiian history, *'ulu* timber was in great demand, to use for surfboards, *pahu* drums and the gunwales of canoes. It is interesting to note that the Hawaiians first used the green breadfruit or disc-shaped slices of the fruit to roll between stakes in their game of *'ulu maika.'* Maybe because of its rough treatment and low rate of survival, breadfruit was later replaced by discs made from stone in the shape of a slice through the center of a firm, green breadfruit.

Breadfruit is served mainly as a vegetable, and it must be either baked, boiled or cooked over charcoal fire unless thrown into the *imu* to steam. It is best cooked when just beginning to turn soft to the touch. Depending on the size, it usually takes about an hour or little more to cook properly in a 350° oven. Breadfruit tends to be stringy if undercooked. You may find that breadfruit is definitely an acquired taste, but a sweet baked *'ulu* smothered in butter is something very special.

If you like breadfruit sweet, wait until the breadfruit is very soft, then bake it. Always add a little water to the baking pan to keep from burning and to create a steaming effect. If you like boiled breadfruit, peel and cut and boil as you would potatoes. Season with salt and pepper and butter and serve hot. For some reason the red Hawaiian salt adds a better flavor. Boiled, baked or steamed, the pulp can be mashed to form into patties and fried in butter until golden brown on both sides.

If you use breadfruit as potatoes in a stew, boil it first, then add to the stew when almost done.

Bake ripe *'ulu* whole in a pan lined with aluminum foil in 350° oven for 1 hour or until done. Opening a cooked breadfruit can be a rather messy operation. Remove fruit from oven and place on sheets of newspaper, pull out the stem and core and cut in half or chunks and season with butter, salt and pepper. Or remove pulp, mash and season to taste.

After steaming the *'ulu* in the *imu*, natives pounded the pulp into poi *'ulu*, much like converting taro into poi, only a much easier procedure. Poi *'ulu* tends to sour faster than poi. Often it was combined with taro poi, maybe to stretch for a large family.

Because of its starch content, breadfruit was fed to pigs being fattened for a royal lu'au in olden days. Wild chickens today love it.

Believe it or not, green breadfruit, when cooked properly and served as a *pupu*, tastes exactly like the heart of an artichoke. Select green breadfruit about the size of a baseball and boil for a long time until tender. Peel, cut into cubes and serve cold with a dipping sauce.

Or serve this as a first course with a spicy catsup dressing. Or even add to a tossed salad.

If you think potato chips are habit forming, you haven't tried BREADFRUIT CHIPS!

Cut a scrubbed, raw green breadfruit in quarters or sixths.

Peel and remove large core. Put in a bowl with ice cubes and refrigerate until thoroughly chilled (overnight is best). Then slice as thin as possible... the thinner the better... and return to the ice water.

Heat oil in deep fryer to 395°. Dry a few slices at a time and drop into the hot oil. Fry until golden brown, drain on absorbent paper, and salt immediately. Store in airtight containers in refrigerator, or freeze.

Carambola

The carambola tree in full bloom with feathery blossoms promises a future crop of waxy, golden-yellow to orange fruit in late summer and during the fall holidays. As kids, we always referred to it as the star fruit tree because the slices looked exactly like stars!

The translucent fruit is 4 to 5 inches long and about 2 inches in diameter, with five distinct ribs, green to yellowish, waxy, thin skin and a crispy, juicy pulp around a core of small brown seeds. The fruit is best eaten raw and doesn't need to be peeled, but I usually trim off the rather tough part of the ribs. The fruit has a mild flavor somewhat like an orange and is usually sweet, but it can be a bit sour.

Unfortunately, most people are not familiar with the value of this fruit, which is consequently just left to rot on the ground. The distinct shape of the slices of the juicy pulp makes them a pretty addition to salads, fruit compotes and floating in exotic drinks.

Carambola can be pickled, used in preserves, or made into juice.

The fruit contains about 10 percent sugar but doesn't have enough pectin for jelly.

To make the juice, chop the fruit into a food processor and then strain the mixture and combine it with water and sugar for a refreshing drink served over ice.

The fruit can be used in stunning holiday table arrangements.

Slices of carambola on a roasting chicken or pork roast add a new dimension.

CARAMBOLA PICKLES

6 c green carambola slices,
cut crosswise 1/4-inch thick
1-1/2 c vinegar
1-1/2 c water

1-3/4 c sugar
1 tablespoon whole cloves
1 stick cinnamon

Combine all but fruit in a large pot and simmer for 10 minutes Add fruit slices, cover and simmer for 45 minutes. Remove cover and cook for approximately 20 minutes or until fruit is tender. Pour into hot, sterilized jars and seal.

DRIED CARAMBOLA

Wash and slice fruit in 1/4-inch thick slices and place in dehydrator or outside drying box to dry in the sun. Store in airtight container when completely dehydrated.

Add slices of carambola to glasses of iced tea instead of slices of lemon.

Coconut

Coconut or *niu* trees have been waving in Hawaiian skies ever since the early immigrating Polynesians brought the sprouting nuts in their double-hull canoes and planted groves of trees. Today waving coco palms are synonymous with the romance of the tropics. Referred to as one of the most useful trees in the world, food was considered the coco palm's least important use.

The coconut tree played a big part in the early Hawaiian way of life. Every part of the palm was put to some use. Native Hawaiians used the fiber to make cordage, mats and brushes, and Island lore tells us that the Hawaiian god Maui snared the sun with cords of sennit, the line produced from coconut fiber. Different parts of the trunk were valuable in the construction of small canoes and posts for houses, and the making of calabashes to hold large portions of food, and hula drums. The leaves were used for thatching and screening houses or temporary shelters, baskets, hats and fans.

The rib fronds were used to string *kukui* nut kernels for lights or flowers for decorations, and when dried made good kindling. Frugal *tutu* made useful brooms from the sturdy ribs.

Today the prized fluted coconut bowls that held generous helpings of poi are considered antiques and demand a high price. Smaller bowls for eating and drinking water were also made from the shells of the nut but are rarely brought out except for small, special poi suppers.

A modern touch was the production of copra for its oil and the meat shipped to markets to be used in baking and as a flavoring. Coconut buttons made from the shell were once the rage in Hawai'i but seldom seen today.

Coconuts were taken on long sea trips or on overland treks instead of regular water as the niu water, was considered more nutritious and germfree.

The water inside the nut is not coconut milk. Milk is the liquid that is made by squeezing the juices out of freshly grated coconut. (Mix 4 cups freshly grated coconut with 2 cups boiling water, let stand 10 minutes, then strain through double thickness of cheesecloth. Squeeze it several times to extract as much liquid as possible. Refrigerate.) This rich cream is the ultimate in flavor, especially in curries.

The old Hawaiians used this basic cream as the main ingredient for puddings mixed with breadfruit, taro, or sweet potato, or thickened it with arrowroot to make *haupia*.

The commercial coconut oil that is found in the market today harks back to the olden days when fair maidens chewed the meat of the nuts, rubbed it through their hair, then played in the surf to wash out the flecks. Oil extracted from the meat was mixed with *maile* leaves or other fragrant plants to make a fine body oil to use in the *lomi-lomi* or for the hair.

Since the Hawaiians used so much coconut, they invented a deluxe grater once the *haole* brought metal to the Islands. A narrow metal piece of steel about 9 inches long with one end flattened and slightly curved upward with teeth was secured on to a straight piece of wood.

As a kid, it was my job to grate the coconut when my mother needed the all-important fresh coconut. Seated firmly on a chair with the board of the grater anchored beneath me and a big wooden bowl placed strategically below the grater, I grasped a half of a cracked coconut with both hands and bore down hard on the grater. It became really fascinating work to make longer and longer strands of pure white meat and to stop grating before specks of brown invaded the pristine shreds of white in the big bowl. I always threatened to clean up the half shell that was left and make my very own coconut cup… but never did.

The most popular way of cracking open a coconut to pry out the white meat is to first drain out the water by poking the two eyes with an ice pick or nail. Then take a hammer and tap around the nut until it is cracked and opens when you drop it on a hard surface.

An alternative method is to place the nut in a 350° oven for an hour and, when you hear it crack, remove the nut. Put it under cold water, tap with a hammer to open and then remove large pieces of meat from the fragmented shell. The chunks of meat are ready to grate or chop only after all the dark skin has been removed.

Today, many coconut groves are losing trees from old age. Even towering trees cannot withstand the ravages of storms and disease, and there is the ever-present problem of public liability from falling nuts and the cost of clipping the leaves and nuts. There aren't many eager young lads around to shimmy up the tree and toss down the choice nuts.

Sprouting coconuts make stunning arrangements in the house or even on a lu'au table.

A medium-sized coconut usually yields 2 to 3 cups of grated meat.

Add grated coconut and sliced bananas to a boxed vanilla cream pie, pour into prepared pie shell and top with whipped cream and more grated coconut.

Curry isn't curry unless you use coconut cream in the sauce and freshly grated coconut for a condiment. Many Islanders use coconut cream instead of milk in curry sauce.

If you have to use the concentrated frozen coconut milk, turn the contents of the can into a strainer placed over a bowl and let it drain overnight in the refrigerator. Spoon off the thick cream that remains in the strainer and use for richer coconut cream.

Slit a cooked sweet potato, add a pat of butter or oleo and sprinkle generously with shredded coconut. Return to oven for 5 minutes to brown the coconut.

Sprinkle freshly grated coconut over an island fruit cocktail or salad.

Toss the leftover shreds of coconut from the final extraction of the liquid onto a baking sheet. Leave in 350° oven for about 10 minutes or until golden brown. Use over ice cream or fruit salads.

The young coconuts or 'spoon' coconuts are delicious. Chop off the top, pierce through the two eyes, chill and sip the liquid through a straw. Then whack the nut in half with a machete and eat the soft custard-like meat with a spoon. Really *ono*!!

Remember the fruit is available the year round for making coconut chips, syrup, candy and numerous baked goods.

COCONUT PUDDING

1-1/2 c coconut milk or plain milk	2 egg whites, beaten
3 tablespoons sugar	1/2 c coconut, grated
2 tablespoons cornstarch	

Heat milk, add sugar and cornstarch mixed with a little water to form a paste and stir well. When it begins to boil and thicken, add egg whites. Cool and add coconut, mix well and pour into mold. Chill to serve.

HAUPIA

2 coconuts, grated	1-1/2 c sugar
4-1/2 c boiling water	1 c cornstarch
1/2 c fresh milk	

Pour boiling water over coconuts and let stand for about 20 minutes. Strain through cloth. Cook the strained mixture over medium heat just up to boiling point, but do not boil. Combine milk, sugar and cornstarch until smooth. Add this mixture to the coconut mixture slowly, stirring constantly until it thickens. Let it cook a few minutes longer. Pour into square pans, and cool until set.

COCONUT SHORTBREAD COOKIES

1 c butter	1 c coconut, grated
3 tablespoons sugar	1 teaspoon vanilla
2 c flour, sifted	

Cream butter and sugar, add rest of ingredients and mix well.

Form into two rolls as for icebox cookies, wrap in wax paper and thoroughly chill. Slice 1/4 inch thick and bake for 30 to 35 minutes in 300° oven on ungreased cookie sheet. Remove while warm and sprinkle with sifted powdered sugar.

COCONUT CAKE

Yellow cake mix	1 box confectioners' sugar, sifted
Carton sour cream	

Follow directions of boxed yellow cake mix and bake in two layer pans. Fill and top with a carton of sour cream mixed with a box of sifted confectioners' powdered sugar, and sprinkle all over generously with freshly grated coconut. Keep refrigerated. It's worth grating fresh coconut!

COCONUT CAKE (USING FRESH COCONUT ONLY)

Prepare one package white cake mix according to package directions and bake in two round layer pans.

Haupia Filling

Mix 6 tablespoons each cornstarch and sugar in a saucepan, add 1/2 cup water and a 14-oz. can frozen coconut milk, thawed. Cook over medium heat, stirring constantly until mixture thickens. Remove from heat and cool slightly. Spread *haupia* filling between the layers of the cake and let cool until firm in refrigerator.

Several hours before serving, whip 1 cup heavy cream with 2 tablespoons sugar and 1/2 teaspoon vanilla until stiff peaks form. Spread the cream over top and sides of cake to completely cover. Sprinkle freshly grated coconut over top and sides... generously!!!

COCONUT CREAM PIE

1 prepared pie crust	1/4 c freshly coconut, grated
4 egg yolks	1 tablespoon butter
1/2 c sugar	pinch of salt
2 c milk	vanilla to flavor
2 heaping T cornstarch	

Place milk, sugar, salt and grated coconut in saucepan. Let come to a boil. Mix cornstarch and egg yolks together with a little water and add to milk mixture. Stir continually until thick on a low flame. Add butter and vanilla. Cool and fill in pie shell. Top with meringue.

Meringue

4 to 6 egg white	grated coconut
approximately 1 tablespoon	
sugar for each egg white	

Beat egg whites until stiff but not dry. Add sugar gradually. Spread over cooled filling, sealing the edges of pastry. Sprinkle coconut over top. Brown in oven.

WAIKIKI COCONUT CREAM PIE

1 prepared baked pie shell	3 tablespoons cornstarch
2 c milk	1/2 teaspoon vanilla
3 egg yolks	1/2 c whipping cream
1/2 c sugar	3/4 c coconut, freshly grated
1/16 teaspoon salt	

Combine sugar, cornstarch, salt. Scald milk and add dry ingredients slowly to hot milk and stir until smooth. Cook over hot water, stirring frequently and cool to lukewarm. Stir in egg yolks. Continue cooking over hot water until custard thickens. Cool, add vanilla and pour into prepared baked pie shell.

Whip chilled cream. Just before serving, spread whipped cream over custard and sprinkle with fresh coconut.

Carrot Cake with Coconut
Stir all together in large bowl:

2 c brown sugar	2 c flour
1 c pineapple, crushed	2 teaspoons baking soda
2 c carrots, well-packed and grated	1/2 teaspoon cinnamon
1/2 c oil	1 teaspoon vanilla
1 c coconut, grated	pinch of salt
1 c nuts, chopped	

Mix well, pour in a greased loaf pan and bake in 350° oven for 45 minutes or when toothpick comes out clean.

Icing
In pan, mix:

1 c sugar	1 tablespoon Karo or pancake syrup
1/2 stick oleo	1/2 c coconut milk or regular milk

Boil 5 minutes to dissolve sugar. Let stand several minutes, then pour over warm cake.

Hawaiian Curry
Fry 1/4 cup sliced onions and 4 cloves minced garlic in 6 tablespoons oleo until browned. Add 6 tablespoons flour, 4 teaspoons curry powder or to taste, 1-1/2 teaspoons salt, 2 teaspoons grated ginger and stir until well blended and smooth.

Gradually add 3/4 cup each milk and chicken broth, stirring constantly until sauce is very thick. Add 1-1/2 cups coconut milk and stir well. Check seasoning and add 4 cups deboned chicken. Thin with broth if necessary.

Serve with rice and the following condiments: mango chutney, grated coconut, chopped peanuts, crumbled crisp bacon, finely chopped hard-boiled eggs, chopped green onions and green peppers, sweet relish, raisins and sliced bananas.

Serve with either a big tossed green salad or Chinese peas.

Haupia Pumpkin Pie
Combine: 1 pound canned pumpkin and 2 slightly beaten eggs.

Stir in: 3/4 cup sugar, 1/2 teaspoon salt and 1 teaspoon cinnamon, 1/2 teaspoon ginger, 1/4 teaspoon cloves.

Stir in one can evaporated milk and 1 cup freshly grated coconut.

Pour into pie shell, bake for 15 minutes in 425° oven. Lower heat to 350° and bake for 40 to 45 minutes more or until filling is set. Cool.

Prepare one package *haupia* pudding mix according to instructions and cool slightly. Pour over cooled pie and chill until firm.

Just before serving, whip 1 cup whipping cream and stir in 1 tablespoon sugar and spread on pie. Sprinkle with 1/2 cup shredded coconut. Refrigerate.

Coconut Candy

3 c sugar
3/4 c milk
3 c fresh coconut, grated

pinch of salt
1 teaspoon white vinegar

Bring sugar and milk to rolling boil, add coconut and rest of ingredients. Cook until soft-ball stage, remove from fire, add vanilla and beat until ready to drop by teaspoonful on waxed paper.

The secret to making good coconut candy is the amount of creaming. If you don't cream it enough, the candy will be soggy and sticky; if you cream too much, the sugar will crystallize and the candy won't be creamy.

For variety, add food coloring to tint a batch pink, light green or yellow.

Old-timer's Coconut Candy

Husk and crack shell of coconut, reserving juice, remove meat from shell and pare off the rind. Grate on medium fine grater.

Combine: 1 cup grated coconut, 1 cup sugar, 2 tablespoons coconut juice (water if necessary) and a pinch of cream of tartar. The mixture will be very thick until the sugar begins to melt.

Heat slowly until it comes to a good boil, then cook 3-1/2 minutes.

Pour onto a flat dinner plate and cream with a fork until it just begins to thicken. Drop quickly by teaspoonful on waxed paper and allow to set.

A drop of coloring may be added just before creaming.

If you like, add a drop or two of peppermint extract for one of the batches. The secret is the amount of creaming.

Uncle Clifford's Coconut Fritters

Pour 3 cups milk over one grated coconut and bring this just to the boil. Add 1/4 to 1/2 cup sugar and a pinch of salt and a teaspoon of vanilla.

Mix 3 heaping tablespoons cornstarch with 1 cup cold milk. Pour mix into coconut mixture and heat until thick, stirring well. Pour into 1-inch deep pan and cool until firm.

Cut into squares, dip in a batter of flour, milk and egg; roll in bread crumbs and fry in deep fat. Remove to absorbent paper and serve hot with maple syrup.

Lazy Man's Frosting for Coconut Cake

Mix up a carton of sour cream with a box of confectioners' powdered sugar, add 2 cups of thawed frozen shredded coconut and mix well to frost a plain layer cake.

Ginger

When the word ginger is mentioned, most people think of exotic white and yellow patches of ginger abounding in the damp valleys for fragrant ginger lei and waxy floral arrangements. On the other hand, people who love to cook picture an odd-looking, irregular-shaped, knobby root with large plump hands and smooth shiny skin that gives a special character to many Island dishes, Oriental cooking, chutneys, curries and teriyaki sauces.

Ginger the flower, and ginger the root do not come from the same plant. Edible ginger is an annual crop raised for its roots. It is distinguished from heartier, leafy flowering ginger by its thin cane-like stalks ranging from 15 to 36 inches tall, depending on the variety, and small red flowers appearing from the stalk about a foot above the ground. When the leaves turn yellow and dry, it is time to harvest the mature roots. However, the immature, pink, young roots with soft skin can be harvested earlier and are excellent for pickling, preserving and making candied or crystallized ginger.

Old Hawaiian cookbooks referred to a 'finger of ginger' which meant about the size of your thumb or index finger, or '5 cents worth' which is anybody's guess at the present prices for ginger.

Originally a native of tropical Asia, ginger has a history in cookery going back to the ancient civilization of India and China.

In Chinese cooking, fresh ginger is used with meat or seafood, and Indian cuisine include fresh ginger in curries, chutneys and other exotic fare. The English came up with a ginger beer, and we in America have ginger ale made from the ginger syrup.

Although ginger is not indigenous to Hawai'i, fresh piquant ginger root is a must in every well-stocked Island kitchen; but remember that ginger is a very strong spice. So start with a small amount and keep tasting until the desired potency is reached. If you add large hunks of ginger to a dish, especially soups and stews, be sure and remove them before serving.

When selecting fresh ginger, look for a root that is firm, without soft spots and with 'thumbs' that can be easily broken off. It will keep in the refrigerator, well wrapped, for several weeks. To use ginger, cut off the amount you'll need, store the rest in the refrigerator and scrape off the dry outside skin. Some people contend that you destroy all the goodness by removing skins, so don't peel or scrape, but scrub the skin well then chop, sliver, grate or squeeze through garlic press for juice. I prefer the latter way of handling.

Hands of ginger may be frozen in ziplock bags, but tend to become soft, which is good for extracting juice. Or it can be cut in chunks to throw into soups.

Bottled ground ginger can be used in entrees or vegetable dishes but lacks the 'zip' of the fresh. However, ground ginger is better used in cakes or where fresh ginger wouldn't be acceptable. One tablespoon fresh ginger juice equals approximately 3/4 teaspoon of the ground variety.

To preserve fresh ginger longer, put the root in a jar with a tight-fitting lid and cover with either vinegar or sherry and refrigerate. This will keep for at least 3 months and the ginger won't absorb the vinegar or sherry flavor but will retain its own zippy taste. The liquid can be added to dishes that need a spicy accent. Add the liquid to mayonnaise along with some of the ginger, minced.

Preserved Ginger: scrub young ginger and either leave in large chunks or slice. Boil in water to cover until the root can be easily pierced. Set aside. For the syrup: for each pound of ginger, allow equal amount of sugar and 1/2 teaspoon cream of tartar and 1/2 pint of water to each pound of sugar. Boil the sugar mixture and simmer to a heavy syrup, skimming off the scum. When the syrup is thick, add the cooked ginger, boil up well and seal in jars.

This preserved ginger is delicious sliced into melted vanilla ice cream and then frozen again. Or slice it very thin and add to fresh fruit cocktails for dessert. Chopped, it makes a lively condiment for curries.

Add a bit of grated fresh ginger to the guava jam pot for an added zip.

For sandwiches, mix three-fourths of a 7-ounce jar of preserved ginger in syrup that has been finely chopped to one softened 8 ounce package of cream cheese. Add the syrup to moisten and flavor until it reaches spreading consistency. Spread evenly on thin slices of buttered bread.

Julie's Ginger Sauce is handy to keep in the refrigerator to serve over ice cream or angel food cake for a last-minute company dessert. Drain one 7-ounce jar preserved ginger, chop ginger very fine and combine again with syrup and about 1/2 cup or more of maple syrup or to taste. Refrigerate.

GINGER-SOY MARINADE

1/2 c soy
1/3 c honey or maple syrup
1/3 c medium dry sherry

1 clove garlic, mashed
1 teaspoon fresh ginger root, grated

Simmer the above ingredients for 5 minutes, then cool. Marinate chicken or pork chops for 4 hours, and baste with marinade while grilling.

TERIYAKI STEAK MARINADE

1 c raw sugar 1 clove garlic, grated
1/4 c sauterne 1 teaspoon ginger, grated

Combine ingredients, simmer until sugar is melted and cool.

MAE'S MELON AND GINGER JAM

3 lbs. Chinese melon juice of one lemon
1/2 c water 1/2 lemon, thinly sliced
1 thumb ginger, finely chopped

Cut melon into very small dices, 1/4 inch or less, add the water and simmer for an hour, stirring at first. As the melon simmers, add an the ginger. Measure the melon and add equal amount of sugar. Stir in the lemon juice and slices and boil all together until the jam jells. Pour in sterilized jars, top with paraffin and securely cover with tops.

GINGER MELON

Slice, peel and cube a white melon. Slice thinly 5 or 6 pieces of bottled ginger in syrup and add to melon together with some of the syrup. Add about 1 tablespoon lemon juice and mix all together. Cover and chill several hours before serving. Garnish with a sprig of mint.

Guava

The guava plant adapted so well to the Hawaiian soil and climate that by 1850 guavas were growing wild in the mountains. Because of its flavor and aroma, the fruit became a great favorite of the natives, and today guavas are the most common wild fruit in the state of Hawai'i.

Guavas still grow wild along the roads and in the mountains today, in spite of progress, and are accessible to those hardy ones who stand ready to pick and enjoy or to the young hikers who revel in good old guava fights... the softer, the better! Generations of Islanders have experimented with the wild fruit for its juice, nectar, jams and jellies and in combination with other fruits.

In 1960 a seedling found in Halemano, O'ahu, was named for John B. Beaumont, a horticulturist and director of the University of Hawai'i Agricultural Department. Today, the larger, robust yellow fruit with pink-colored pulp and seeds provides 5 to 6 ounces of juice per fruit in contrast to the 2 to 3 ounces from the wild variety. If you have the room in your garden, it might be worth it to plant a few of these Beaumont guavas. This will save you foraging time, and half the amount of fruit makes a great jelly.

There are several varieties of the common guava... the sour red, the sweet white and the small strawberry, or what old-timers referred to as "Wi-wi." Landscape artists use the latter extensively because of its beautiful bark and shape. Strawberry guavas grow wild but are tedious to pick and stew up for jelly. However, the ruby-red color and sweet flavor is worth it all.

Guavas can be either sweet or tart and acidy, but are high in vitamin C. By freezing the guava juice and pulp when it is fresh and plentiful, you may enjoy the fruit in many different ways all year round.

Pick only firm ripe guavas, and more importantly some half ripe-to-green ones of good quality for the pectin. Don't bother with the really soft ones. To prepare: wash, cut off stem and blossom ends and slice into large aluminum, stainless steel or enamel pot. The less water you add when cooking the fruit, the shorter the cooking time and lighter the finished jelly. So bring the water just up to where you can just see it below the top layer of guavas, bring to a boil, then simmer gently until the fruit is mushy, stirring often so it won't stick to the bottom and burn.

For clear jelly, pour this into jelly bags, suspend over large containers and be patient until it drips dry… don't squeeze the bag! Or extract the juice by lining an enameled colander with cheesecloth and let it drip. If you are in a hurry and want a jelly/jam, strain and mash this cooked fruit through a colander or ricer for a thin purée.

Rule of thumb: don't be tempted to cook more than 3 cups of juice at a time for jelly. Two is preferable. Use a large, flat-bottomed pan which will hold four times the amount of juice to be cooked and shorten cooking time. As the jelly should be made quickly, allow the juice to boil vigorously.

Measure a cup of juice for a cup of sugar and stir until sugar is dissolved. Bring to a boil and remove scum as it forms on top and keep as a sweet treat. Some people find it quicker to boil the juice alone for 5 minutes, then stir in the sugar and boil vigorously to dissolve it. Either way, test frequently by dipping the spoon in jelly, then raise it a foot above the pot out of the steam and turn so the syrup runs off the side. When three or four drops run together and 'sheet' off the spoon in one mass, it is done. Remove from heat and pour into hot, sterilized jars, filling to within 1/2 inch from the top and cover immediately with hot melted paraffin.

Place sticks of paraffin in a clean, dry can and put that can in a larger can of water over low heat to melt gradually. It is important to be very careful not to spill the paraffin as it is inflammable. Just a single layer spread evenly over the top of the jelly in the jar is better than a thick layer. Cover glasses with lids or aluminum foil and store in a cool, dry place.

Be sure to wash and rinse the glasses to be used and place in a large pot. Cover with water, bring to a boil and continue boiling at least 20 minutes. Handle carefully when removing from water and drain. Sterilize the covers at the same time.

Don't waste the remaining pulp left in the jelly bag or colander after the juice has dripped. Put this through a sieve or ricer for clear purée which is now ready for freezing or making jam.

Jam: mix 3 cups each guava pulp and sugar and cook slowly, stirring frequently to keep from burning, until it thickens and sheets.

For a tasty variety, add grated ginger or dashes of cinnamon, mace and allspice. Or add a few slivered slices of fresh limes, Chinese orange or kumquats… careful, no seeds!

The purée is apt to bubble and splatter over you and the stove, so best you cover the pot and protect your hands and arms when stirring. I use a clean dishtowel to wrap around my arm.

Place a spoonful of guava jelly in the bottom of the cup before adding custard.

For a sandwich, combine guava jelly with chunky peanut butter.

Use part guava juice for liquid while stewing prunes.

Guava wood makes an excellent charcoal for barbecuing.

Old-timers still recommend chewing the tender young shoots of the guava to relieve diarrhea.

For plain Guava Marmalade, slice 2-1/2 cups guava rind and combine with 2 cups juice and bring to a boil. Add 2 cups sugar, tablespoon lemon juice and boil hard until it jells. Keep stirring so rind doesn't burn on bottom. Pour into sterile bottles.

Guava Relish might take a little time but can be used in several ways besides with cold meats.

Cut half-ripe and a few green guavas in half and remove every trace of seed (use this in jam later) then slice and chop very small.

Combine 2 cups guava with 2 cups each finely chopped cabbage, green and red bell peppers, round onions and a liberal helping of chopped garlic and as many chopped Hawaiian chili peppers as you dare!

In a pot bring to a boil a little less than a quart of vinegar and 2 cups brown sugar, 2 tablespoons Hawaiian salt, teaspoon each powdered cloves, celery seed, allspice and turmeric, then add the chopped guava and veggies. Add chopped and de-seeded Hawaiian chili peppers to discretion and taste.

Let this simmer down for about 2 hours to a thick consistency, stirring frequently, and bottle in sterilized jars.

Spoon dollops of the relish over a small cube of Philadelphia cream cheese and serve with crackers for pupu. Spicy delight.

You may also use it plain for a dip with bite-sized chunks of avocado.

Or dip the chunks of avocado in cracker crumbs and deep-fry in hot oil to serve hot with the relish.

GUAVA DRESSING

1 c mayonnaise	1 teaspoon dry mustard
1 c tomato catsup	2 teaspoon lemon juice
1/4 c vinegar	1/2 c guava jelly or jam
1/2 c oil	minced garlic, salt and sugar to taste

Combine all in a blender or mix with a beater. Keep refrigerated.

GUAVA BARS

1-1/2 c flour	1/2 c butter or oleo
1/2 teaspoon baking powder	1/2 c sugar
1/2 teaspoon cinnamon	1/2 teaspoon vanilla
1/4 teaspoon ground cloves	1 egg
1/3 c nuts, chopped	3/4 c guava jam

Sift dry ingredients and cut in shortening. Add vanilla to the egg and combine with the flour mixture. Spread two-thirds of the mixture in an oiled 11x7-inch pan. Mix jam and nuts together and spread on crust. Top with remaining flour mixture and bake in 375° oven for 25 minutes. Cool in pan and cut into bars. Makes 24 bars.

Guava Cheese Cake

1 8-oz. plus 1 3-oz. cream cheese, softened   1/2 c sugar
2 eggs, slightly beaten   1 teaspoon vanilla

Beat ingredients until smooth. Pour into 9-inch prepared graham cracker crust and bake for 20 minutes in 350° oven. Cool.

Add Topping: 1/2 cup sugar, juice of 1/2 lemon, 1-1/2 tablespoons cornstarch and one can frozen guava juice. Combine and cook until thickened. Cool and spread over cheese cake. Keep refrigerated until serving.

Crust: Combine 1-1/4 cups graham cracker crumbs, 3 tablespoons sugar and 1/4 cup melted butter. Press mixture into bottom and sides of 9-inch pan and bake in 350° oven for 10 minutes or until lightly browned.

Guava Oatmeal Squares

In a bowl sift 1 cup flour, 1/2 teaspoon each salt and soda. Add 1/2 cup brown sugar and cut in 1/2 cup shortening until consistency of cornmeal. Add 1 cup rolled oats, blend well and press half of mixture into oiled 7x11-inch pan.

Combine 1 cup guava pulp, 1/3 cup sugar, 2 teaspoons lemon juice and 1/2 cup chopped nuts and spread over crumb mixture. Top with remaining crumb mixture and bake in 350° oven for 40 minutes. Cool in pan and then cut in squares.

Guava Ice

Mix together 2 cups guava purée, 2 tablespoons lime or lemon juice, 1 cup sugar or more if guavas are very sour, 3 tablespoons Pream dissolved in 1/2 cup warm water. Stir well and freeze. When it is mushy, beat and return to freezer.

If you have some guava jelly that didn't jell, don't despair. Fry up sliced bananas until nicely browned in butter, turn into casserole and drizzle the guava jelly to coat, and top with a jigger or two of rum. Serve warm with whipped cream or ice cream for dessert.

Melt guava jelly down and use for glaze on ham.

Pick a bag full of fresh guavas, leave them on the table and enjoy their luscious taste… and store up on vitamin C!

Pile crushed ice in plastic cups and pour guava juice over all. Leave these in the freezer compartment for the junior traffic to enjoy!

Kukui

As you look up into the lush green valleys, the patches of lighter green cascading down the mountainside are *kukui* trees which have sprouted in a sprawling pattern from the fallen nuts of the trees. These trees thrive in the lower, woody areas of the mountains, gulches and valleys.

The *kukui* nut trees were mentioned in old Hawaiian legends and the Menehune are reputed to have used the nuts for tops. The ancient Hawaiians considered *kukui* one of their most versatile plants. The kernels were used for light and fuel, ornaments, relishes, and medicine, and dyes for tapa and tattoos. Canoes were made from the trunks of trees.

The early Hawaiians made torches from stalks of bamboo stuffed with roasted kernels of *kukui* nuts and ignited.

Roasted or sun-dried kernels were strung on pieces of the coconut midrib and used as candles. Lamps were made by placing *kukui* nut oil in the hollow of a stone.

The meat of the raw *kukui* nuts was used as a strong cathartic and, mashed, the Hawaiians used it in enemas.

Today, the nuts are polished and strung in lei and bracelets and made into earrings. The lei of the leaves and flowers are representative of the island of Molokai, especially when worn in parades.

We were brought up with the old Hawaiian superstition that it was bad luck to plant *kukui* trees in your yard, until one day the myth was finally exploded. It seems that an old *tutu* asked her *kane* to plant a *kukui* tree in the yard, and the lazy fellow excused himself by convincing her that it was bad luck!

So now we have several trees in the garden. Strangely enough, the light-green leaves vary greatly in shape and size and have an underside of silvery gray down or powder. The delicate, pale, creamy-white five-petalled flowers grow in clusters, and as a child I always thought that maybe the Menehune strung them into lei.

We have experimented with the art of topiary gardening on potted *kukui* trees and enjoyed them on the lanai until they outgrew the pots, and for the past 15 years we have had fun training one of the trees we planted just over a hillside. As a result of weighing branches down with rocks and pruning shoots, there are now two 5-foot limbs that stretch out on either side of the sturdy but stunted trunk.

In the 1930s Paul Fagan bought Pu'uohoku Ranch on the eastern end of Molokai which included one of the most sacred *heiau* in the Islands. Mrs. Fagan had the greatest respect for the sacred Kukui Grove and was adamant that we enter the grove quietly, with great reverence, and walk carefully between the trees so as not to disturb anything or break even a twig. We abided by her beliefs and wishes and maintained an almost holy silence when entering.

Unfortunately, a *malihini* houseguest disregarded the tabu while in this hallowed Hawaiian spot and that evening suffered severe back pains and had to be sent to Honolulu on a stretcher for medical treatment. Superstitious or not, we have been reluctant to enter the Kukui Grove after that, content just to peer into the eerie interior.

The many uses of the *kukui* tree for oil, light, food and medicine have been handed down from generation to generation by *kupuna*, so all is not lost. I remember my grandmother gathering the hard, wrinkly nuts and baking them in a huge pan in the oven, then cracking each one with a hammer, removing the oily kernel and chopping it up for *inamona*, which she always kept in the icebox.

The *kukui* nut, shaped like an English walnut, can still be found today if you care to make your own *inamona*, but you may also buy balls of *kukui* nut already prepared in the markets where Hawaiian foods are sold. Be sure and gather only the perfect nuts and discard any that smell bad or are riddled with ants.

Use as a condiment, especially with raw fish.

Roast the whole *kukui* nut slowly in the oven for at least 30 minutes until brown, crack open and remove kernel of meat. Pound with a rock or blunt end of a knife... don't chop... add a pinch of Hawaiian salt and fry for few minutes, then bottle. Keep refrigerated.

If you want to oil your priceless calabashes, don't fry the meat, just put it in cheesecloth securely and rub the bowls the way the old Hawaiians did.

Never, never, never eat the raw nut!!!

Kumquat

Kumquats rate high on the list of the more exotic citrus found in the Islands. This small orange-like fruit was brought to Hawai'i originally before 1880 from China and planted in Island gardens more as an ornamental plant. The bushy tree, covered with the glossy, miniature, oval-shaped golden oranges with a smooth skin, created quite a lovely picture to enjoy for the few weeks they were in season. Then they simply rotted and fell to the ground. It wasn't until the Asian people immigrated to the Islands in the 1880s and brought their devotion to the kumquat with them that a demand for the fruit was created. Strangely enough, kumquats are not listed in early Hawaiian cookbooks.

Kumquats were part of the culture of China and honored by royalty and peasants alike. Bowls of kumquats or *chin kan*, the Golden Orange, were placed at the foot of the great Buddha. The Orientals never cooked the fruit but preserved the whole orange in honey for about a week or two until the fruit was transparent. Then it was served cold as an after-dinner delicacy.

If you'd like a tart surprise, rub the ripe fruit briskly until it fairly glows, then pop it in your mouth and chew. The spicy, sweet peel and tart pulp of this tiny fruit is big on flavor. People don't really appreciate the many potentials of the kumquat. It makes the best marmalade and candied fruit or it can be preserved whole in a thick syrup.

Bottle the leftover juice and serve as a syrup over ice cream, waffles, or pancakes, add to fruit cocktails or it's delicious to baste a pork roast with.

Thinly sliced kumquats may be added to salads, compotes, and even vegetables for a tangy surprise. Try a slice of kumquat instead of lemon in your tea. The many potentials are quite unique in flavor and texture. Kumquats may be small and a bit more trouble to prepare, but so worth the trouble.

We enjoyed a potted kumquat tree on the lanai until it outgrew the pot, so we planted it in the garden where we can enjoy watching the ripening fruit and reap the harvest it can bring!

KUMQUAT MARMALADE

3 qts water

2 c kumquats, seeded and
    thinly sliced, about 24

1-1/2 c orange pulp, chopped

1-1/2 c orange peel,
    about 2 medium oranges, sliced

1/2 c lemon juice

9 c sugar

Add water to fruit, cover and let stand in a cool place overnight, then bring to a boil and cook until peel is tender. To each cup of fruit mixture add 1 cup sugar. Stir until sugar is dissolved. Cook rapidly and keep testing for jelly, about 45 minutes, stirring occasionally to prevent sticking. Pour boiling hot into hot jars, cover with paraffin and lids. 8-1/2 pints.

KUMQUAT MARMALADE

1 pt. fresh kumquats

4 c water

sugar

1 tablespoon lemon juice

Slice kumquats in paper-thin circles, removing seeds, to measure about 2-1/2 cups of slices. Cover with water and let stand overnight. Boil mixture for 30 minutes, then measure into a 3-quart saucepan. For each cup of fruit mixture, add 1-1/2 cups sugar. Return to heat and cook to a full rolling boil. Boil hard till mixture sheets off the spoon, about 3 minutes. Stir in lemon juice and seal in hot scalded jars. Yields 1 pint.

Instead of tediously removing seeds, skim them off with a slotted spoon while they're cooking!

KUMQUAT JAM

Wash fruit, cut in half crosswise, squirt out seeds and juice into a strainer. Reserve pulp and rind to combine with juice and chop roughly in food processor. For 3 cups pulp, add 3/4 cup water or orange juice and 5 cups sugar. Let it come to a rolling boil, cook slowly and stir occasionally until it sheets from the spoon. Jar and treasure.

Or you may boil the pulp and juice for 20 minutes, then add the sugar all at once and boil for another 15 minutes or until it jells.

KUMQUAT PRESERVES

2 c kumquats

1 c water

2 c sugar

1 stick cinnamon

1 lime, juiced or sliced thin

Cut small gash in each kumquat. Cover with water and bring to a boil, then drain. Bring sugar and water to a boil, drop in kumquats, cinnamon and lime and cook for 10 minutes. Let stand overnight. Next day cook uncovered for 10 minutes. Let stand until cool. Bring to a boil and cook until fruit is transparent and the syrup is thick. Pack into sterilized jars while hot, cover with hot syrup. Seal at once. Or punch each clean kumquat in four places with a large needle. Pour water, kumquats, sugar, ginger and juice into saucepan and simmer till liquid becomes thick and fruit translucent. Seal into several sterilized jars.

CANDIED KUMQUATS

Cut fresh fruit in halves and remove seeds. Cook as for Preserved Kumquats. Remove fruit with a slotted spoon and lay separately on cookie sheets and dry in slow oven. Serve as a confection.

BRANDIED KUMQUATS

3 c kumquats, washed	2 c sugar
1-1/2 teaspoons baking soda	brandy

Sprinkle fruit with baking soda, cover with boiling water and let stand for about 10 minutes. Pour off water and rinse fruit thoroughly. Make two deep slits in each end of kumquats and place in enough cold water to cover. Bring to a boil, cook for 15 minutes more and set aside.

Bring sugar and water to a boil for 5 minutes, add kumquats and cook until fruit is transparent and the syrup is thick. Remove pan from heat and let kumquats plump in the syrup overnight.

Reheat the syrup to boiling and pack kumquats in clean, sterilized jars. Add 1 to 3 tablespoons of your best brandy to each 1/2-pint jar. Pour hot syrup over the fruit to fill the jars to within 1/2 inch of top and seal. Makes 3 to 4 pints.

GINGERED KUMQUATS

4 c kumquats, washed well	1 c water
2 c sugar	2 tablespoons fresh ginger, grated

Boil all ingredients except kumquats together for 5 minutes, add kumquats and cook in a covered pan over low heat for 45 minutes or until tender. Stir occasionally. Makes about 1 quart or 2 pint jars.

CHICKEN WITH KUMQUAT

Marinate 5 to 6 pounds of chicken thighs for 6 hours in following sauce: 1/2 cup dry white wine, 1/4 cup each lime juice and soy, 1 cup chopped onions, 4 cloves crushed garlic, 1 teaspoon each curry and grated ginger. Reserve marinade. Brown chicken in butter and place in a baking dish. Stir flour into pan drippings until thick, then gradually stir in marinade and cook until bubbly and thickened. Pour sauce over chicken and slice preserved kumquats on top, cover with foil and bake in 350° oven for an hour or until tender.

Liliko'i

Years ago it was as common to see children in Hawai'i with a *liliko'i* protruding from their mouths as pacifiers in children's mouths today! Only, the old folks warned us to chew the seeds so they wouldn't land in our appendix!

Though both are known as water lemons, passion fruit is the sour yellow variety and the purple skinned *liliko'i* is sweeter and harder to find. The prolific vine grows wild in the mountains and is heavy with fruit during summer and fall.

Passion fruit can be a 'run-away' fruit in your garden, but if you have the space, let them run, climb, tangle and take over so you may enjoy the unusual purple flower with a cross-like center that turns into a hard, brittle, yellow-shelled fruit. It can be a pest, but the yellow pulp with many black seeds is loaded with vitamin C. Because of this high acidity, the juice keeps for a long time in the refrigerator.

As you're picking a bucketful, don't bypass the fallen, wrinkled fruit as they become sweeter with age and are perfectly all right. Toss your golden harvest into the sink, wash, cut in half gingerly, as they tend to slip, then scoop out the pulp and black seeds from the spongy white sac.

Either put this through a ricer or squeeze out the juice through several layers of cheesecloth. This can either be stored in the refrigerator or frozen. It is best to freeze only small quantities as the flavor is so potent. The old-fashioned ice trays are the best, as the individual frozen cubes can be stored in ziplock bags and brought out when needed for juice, slushes, pies, and jellies and added to other fruit juices.

If you're using a recipe that calls for cooking the juice, it is best to add the juice near the end of the cooking process.

PASSION FRUIT PUNCH

2 c passion fruit juice
1/2 c orange juice
1/4 c lemon or lime juice
1 c freshly brewed tea

1/2 c sugar
1 pint bottle ginger ale
crushed ice

Combine all but the ginger ale and ice and chill. Just before serving, add the ginger ale and ice. If you're using this recipe for a party, float some passion fruit sherbet in a punch bowl. Allow 1 pint to each gallon of punch. Yields 1-1/2 quarts.

Passion Fruit Jelly

3-1/2 c passion fruit juice 1 bottle liquid pectin
7 c sugar

Combine juice and sugar and bring to a boil. Immediately add the pectin, stirring constantly. Bring again to a full rolling boil for 1/2 minute. Remove from heat, let stand 1 minute, skim, pour quickly into sterilized glasses. Cover with hot melted paraffin. Yields 10 6-oz. glasses.

Passion Fruit Sponge Pudding

4 eggs, separated 1/3 teaspoon salt
2 c sugar 2 tablespoons butter, melted
6 tablespoons passion fruit juice 6 tablespoons enriched flour
2 c milk

Beat egg yolks until thick and lemon-colored; add sugar gradually, beating well after each addition. Add juice and milk, then salt and melted butter. Fold in flour and stiffly beaten egg whites. Pour into a well-oiled 1-1/2-quart baking dish or individual custard cups. Bake in a pan of hot water at 325° for 1 hour or until firm. Loosen edges of pudding; turn out on serving dish with custard on top. 8 servings.

Passion Fruit Chiffon Cake

2-1/4 c cake flour 1/2 c water
1 c sugar 1/4 c passion fruit juice
1 teaspoon salt 1 c egg whites
1 tablespoon baking powder 1/2 teaspoon cream of tartar
1/2 c salad oil 1/2 c sugar
5 egg yolks

Sift flour, the 1 cup sugar, salt and baking powder into mixing bowl. Make a well in the flour and add oil, yolks, water and juice. Beat with a spoon until smooth. Beat egg whites with cream of tartar until whites form soft peaks. Add 1/2 cup sugar gradually, beating after each addition. It's stiff enough when it doesn't slide when bowl is inverted. Gradually pour yolk mixture over meringue, gently folding with rubber spatula until just blended. Pour into an unoiled 10-inch tube pan and bake at 325° for 1 hour. Immediately turn pan upside down on cake rack and let stand until cold. Remove from pan. Serve with *liliko'i* sherbet.

Passion Fruit Chiffon Pie

4 eggs, separated
1 c sugar
1/2 teaspoon salt
1/2 c passion fruit juice
1 tablespoon unflavored gelatin

1/4 c cold water
1 teaspoon lemon rind, grated
1 baked pie shell
1/2 c heavy cream, whipped

Beat egg yolks until thick, add 1/2 cup of the sugar, salt and juice. Cook over low heat until thick, stirring constantly. Soften gelatin in the cold water, add to mixture, stirring until dissolved. Add rind; cool until thickened. Fold in stiffly beaten egg whites to which the remaining 1/2 cup sugar has been added. Pour into pie shell and chill until firm. Serve with whipped cream.

Passion Fruit Parfait Pie

3/4 c passion fruit juice
2 tablespoons sugar
1 package lemon gelatin

1 pint vanilla ice cream
1-1/2 c sweetened applesauce
9" baked pie shell or crumb crust

Heat juice with sugar, remove from heat and add gelatin and stir until dissolved. Add ice cream and stir until melted and blend in applesauce. Chill until mixture begins to thicken. Turn into pie shell and chill. Serve with whipped cream sprinkled with chocolate shavings.

Liliko'i Bread

6 tablespoons butter
3/4 c white sugar
2 eggs
1/4 c milk

1-1/2 c flour
1-1/2 teaspoons baking powder
1/4 teaspoon salt
1/2 c liliko'i concentrate, undiluted

Cream butter and sugar, beat in eggs, add the flour that has been sifted with the baking powder and salt alternately with the milk. Bake in a greased loaf pan for 1 hour at 375°. Remove hot loaf from oven, prick holes all over and dribble the *liliko'i* concentrate over the loaf.

Add a little glamour and zest to your fruit salad platter by scooping out the flesh and seed of *liliko'i* and sprinkling it over the fruit for color.

Limu

Fortunately, the first voyagers to Hawai'i brought along a some-what limited supply of plants and foods, since they found only the *'ohelo* berry, *pepeiao* (a fleshy fungus found on dead bark) and *'akala* berries (a native raspberry) and *limu* abounding in the waters around them.

Having settled along the seashore, these pioneers depended largely on the bounties from the ocean to provide them with food. One of the pre-contact (before Captain Cook) foods was a sea vegetable, seaweed or *limu*. Considered part of a typical Hawaiian meal in the past, it was used as a spice and relish. However, today there are only a few *limu* pickers who have the time or tenacity to comb the reefs and sandy bot-toms at low tide, or even care for the pesky chore of cleaning the *'opala* from the *limu*. It's easier to buy it in the market all nicely cleaned and packaged. Actually, today some varieties of *limu* are considered a deli-cacy and are served sparingly at a lu'au. Originally *limu* was used in religious ceremonies, as a medicine or as food, the spicier ones used sparingly to flavor or accent dishes.

In our *limu*-picking days, we had our favorite spots where we knew just where the *limu* grew and hoarded our secret! Then, at low tide we could dive or crawl along the reef to attack the *limu* beds. Some pre-ferred to pick *limu* from floating masses along the shore, but whatever way one goes after *limu*, you should know what you're picking… like mushrooms!

Even back in the ancient Hawaiian civilization, *limu-kohu* was con-sidered the ultimate in seaweed. This small red to purple *limu* was some-times forbidden to all but *ali'i* and was even cultivated in ocean gar-dens. Today it is still highly prized and rather expensive. So, it is no wonder faithful *limu*-pickers won't disclose their secret *limu-kohu* beds!

If you've ever picked *limu-kohu*, you can easily visualize a forest of tiny, pink pine trees waving in the water. These stalks with tufts of fuzzy branches vary from 1 to 8 inches and grow best where there is a con-stant flow of water, especially along craggy reefs in the surf line. It is tempting to just pull a handful from the rocks between waves, but for the good of the plant the stems should be cut and the roots left to grow anew.

Strangely enough, some seaweeds seem to gravitate to one area, and some seaweeds are found only on one island of the Hawaiian chain;

some are seasonal. But all have to be cleaned thoroughly by picking out the loose sand, coral and *'opala*. It is best to do this tedious chore along the seashore and rinse the seaweed thoroughly in the salt water since fresh water affects the *limu*. Some varieties are soaked 24 hours to remove the bitterness, and others can be eaten the same day. Most can be salted and stored in the refrigerator for several weeks. *Limu* is eaten primarily with meat and fish.

The long, green strands of *limu-ele'ele* are found at the mouth of streams in fresh or brackish water, or in springs, near the water's edge. This *limu* used to be a must for stew; however, today it is like finding gold!

Limu wawae'iole or Rat's Feet is also known as *miru* to the Japanese and *pokpokio* to the Filipinos. This dark-green *limu* is velvety soft to the touch and has a spongy, almost cottony texture. This one is fun to gather and is relatively easy at low tide. Just pull yourself along the sandy or rocky bottom and grope. It grows in the form of a creeping mat over coral rock and sand without definite roots at a depth of 1 to 15 feet. A layer of sand and silt usually covers the plant, making it difficult to locate and dreadful to clean. But, by rubbing it together between your hands in salt water and picking it over, it's not too bad.

When using this *limu* in a salad, the freshly collected *limu* should be rinsed in salt water, then mixed with the dressing immediately before serving, as it wilts very fast. The fresh plant can be refrigerated for only a few days before it softens, wilts and gets rather gelatinous.

Teriyaki Style Limu Waiwae'iole: Wash and clean the *limu* in salt and fresh water, drain and chop in 2-inch lengths. Mix with 3/4 cup prepared teriyaki sauce, 1-1/2 tablespoons sesame seeds and 1/2 cup chopped green onions. Optional: add chopped, de-seeded chili pepper if you like it hot!

The most common and popular *limu* in the Islands is *manauea* or *ogo*, which is enjoyed by all ethnic groups. It grows in coral rubble on reefs, usually in shallow water. Once you harvest a big bag full, the most tedious job is removing the *'opala*. There are many ways to serve this, but the old-time Hawaiians chopped and salted the *limu*, mixed it with other *limu* and used it to thicken chicken and pork stews.

Today *ogo* can be prepared in many ways and, because of its mild taste, is recommended for any beginner *limu*-eater. And remember! *Limu* is high in iodine content!

Incidentally, there is another *limu* that is hard to come by as it grows on the backs of *'opihi* and is known as the *'opihi limu*.

Two of the most popular seaweeds, *limu-kohu* and *manauea*, are eaten with meat, stew especially, and raw fish as a condiment. *Manauea* or *ogo* has a milder flavor and makes a delicious salad.

Manauea Salad

Rinse one bag store-bought *limu manauea* thoroughly then briefly blanch it in boiling water, no more than 2 minutes, and drain well under cold water in a colander. Chop it up and mix it to taste with Hawaiian salt, vinegar, minced chili pepper or chili pepper water, chopped round onions and tomatoes. Keep refrigerated.

Poke

2 lbs. skinned raw *ahi*,
    cut into bite-sized pieces
2 oz. *limu kohu*

1 teaspoon *inamona* (kukui nut)
1 teaspoon Hawaiian salt or to taste

Combine fish, *limu*, *inamona* and salt and let stand 15 minutes. Cover and chill well. Optional: chopped green onions and chili peppers.

Ogo Guacamole

pulp of 2 large avocados,
    coarsely mashed with fork
juice of 1/2 lemon
1 medium tomato, chopped

1 small onion, chopped
1 c ogo, chopped
salt, chili pepper water and corn chips

Combine all ingredients except corn chips, test for seasoning and turn into bowl surrounded with the chips.

Lychee

The Lychee, also spelled litchi, lichee, lichi and leechee, originated in Asia, where it has been popular in southern China for 2,000 years. Lychee trees are now found growing in many countries throughout the world.

The original tree was first brought to Hawai'i by Ching Chock and planted on the Chun Afong property on School and Nuuanu Streets, where the tree stands today in the Chun Hoon Shopping Center. Today, the lychee tree is found in many Island gardens, but does not tolerate strong winds as we found to our great dismay during Hurricane Iniki. However, slowly the trees are coming back in full leaf. So trees are best planted in a protected spot.

The red-brown, rough-skinned fruit resembles a large strawberry, but beneath the shell is a white, juicy, sweet pulp surrounding a small brown pit in the center. Lychees are like peanuts... once you start shelling and eating this exotic fruit, you can't stop!

Before lychee trees became so popular in Hawai'i, lychees were imported dried in fancy red Chinese boxes with lots of gold filigree, especially at Christmastime. Between the discarded shiny pits, tangerine rinds, shells from the lychee and various nuts, and candy, coffee tables could become quite a 'dumping ground' at holiday time. The dried fruit still in the warty, dusky-brown, crinkly shell looks and tastes somewhat like a prune. The flesh shrinks away from the sides of the shell and is amber in color.

Lychee season is short... June and July usually, and the birds, especially the *meijiro* or white eyes, love the lychee when the fruit is bright red and ready for harvesting. It is best to cut the whole branch of hanging fruit clusters to protect the delicate shells from cracking or bruising.

To peel a fresh lychee, remove the stem so as to create a hole to begin peeling off the outer shell. The problem of removing the pits is rather delicate while trying to keep the fruit whole for serving in special dishes. Slice off the stem end with a sharp knife before the fruit is peeled and cut carefully around the pit with the tip of a vegetable peeler and lift it out, careful not to rip the flesh. Not an easy task as the delicate flesh tends to cling to its stone. Once the pit is removed, the shell can be peeled away without danger of damaging the lychee.

Of course, the canned lychees preserved in a thin syrup can't begin to compare with the delicate flavor of the freshly peeled lychee, but, when you need a whole lychee, they are so convenient.

Canned or fresh lychees, whole or sliced, are a great addition to other tropical fruits in a salad or fruit cocktail.

If you freeze lychees, bag a whole cluster, stems and all, instead of freezing the individual fruit. This keeps the fruit intact and the flesh from being exposed. Lychees do tend to lose their fine texture when frozen, but they may be stored for at least a year, or from one season to another!

LYCHEE SALAD

Use Manoa lettuce, butter lettuce or romaine, anything but iceberg.

Make cream cheese balls, or just cut little cubes of cream cheese, and roll in chopped chives, Combine with canned lychees and sliced avocado.

Mix at last minute with your favorite French dressing.

PAKE-HAOLE SALAD

1/2 an avocado per person
1 can lychee or fresh lychee,
   peeled and seeded

1 small can macadamia nuts, chopped
1 bottle of your favorite
   French dressing

Peel avocado, remove seed and spray with lemon juice. Fill each hollow with lychee. Lay on bed of lettuce, sprinkle chopped macadamia nuts on top and pour the dressing over.

MOLDED LYCHEE SALAD RING

1 (10-1/2-oz.) can lychee,
   halved and seeded
1 #303 can grapefruit sections
   or 1 can (11-oz) mandarin oranges

1 tablespoon unflavored gelatin
1 package orange-flavored gelatin
1 package lemon-flavored gelatin

Thoroughly drain canned fruits, saving the liquids, then add enough water to the juices to make 3-1/2 cups. Empty packages of flavored gelatin in a large bowl. Soften the unflavored gelatin in 1/4 cup of the fruit juice mixture. Heat the remaining juice to boiling, add unflavored gelatin and pour over gelatins in the bowl, stirring to dissolve gelatins completely.

Cool thoroughly, add grapefruit or orange and lychees. Pour into a well-oiled 1-quart ring mold and chill until completely set. 8 servings.

Optional: fill center with a choice of chicken salad, seafood salad, slices of avocado or plain cottage cheese, sprinkled with paprika for added color.

Lychee Chicken Salad

2 lbs. chicken breasts, skinned
    and deboned
1-1/2 c water
1 large onion, chopped
1 small piece ginger root, crushed
1 teaspoon salt
1-1/2 teaspoons curry powder
2 cans (11-oz.) Mandarin oranges
    (optional)

1 can (1 lb. 4 oz.) lychee
    or fresh equivalent
2/3 c mayonnaise
1 tablespoon lemon juice
1/2 teaspoon orange rind, grated
lettuce leaves

In a saucepan combine chicken, water, onion, ginger, salt and 1/2 teaspoon of the curry, cover and bring to a boil. Lower heat and simmer for 20 minutes or until chicken is cooked. Cool in stock (use stock for soup later). Cut chicken into chunks.

Drain oranges and lychees, reserving 1 tablespoon of the lychee syrup. Combine chicken, oranges and lychees; chill. Combine mayonnaise, lemon juice and orange rind. Stir in the 1 tablespoon lychee syrup and the remaining 1 teaspoon curry powder. Pour over salad and mix lightly. Serve salad on lettuce leaves. 6 servings.

Mango

Although mangoes are relatively new to the Western world, the fruit has been esteemed in southern Asia for more than 5,000 years and introduced in Hawai'i in only the early 1800s. The varying colors of green and vivid yellows, oranges and reds of the luscious fruit are an inspiration and challenge for artists to capture their glossy beauty.

A noted horticulturist once told a group of garden enthusiasts that one of the most beautiful trees in Hawai'i was the mango, and *kama'aina* tend to agree with him. As I sit writing this, I'm looking across at a stash of mango trees covered with new, light-green, shimmering leaves dappled with a slight tinge of brown, darker russet browns and sharp reddish purple. Soon the yellowish blossoms will appear... and if the winds don't blow... tiny mangoes will begin to form. The whole cycle of the mango tree is a fascinating phenomenon of nature.

Sometimes called the 'king of fruits,' the common mango tree covered with luxuriant green foliage may grow as high as 70 feet. We kids thought mango trees were made for climbing and tree houses or forts, and the fruit to eat green with soy!

A seasonal fruit, mangoes usually begin to ripen in April and continue through the summer months into October, and do best in hot, dry leeward areas. Unfortunately, mango, like poison ivy, has an allergic reaction in some people and can cause an unpleasant rash. As children, we were always taught to wash our face and hands thoroughly after gorging on mangoes over the sink... the only way to truly enjoy ripe, juicy mangoes! But then the fibers that cling to the hairy seed proved a bit of a dental problem.

Mangoes may be a rich source of vitamin A and C, but they are full of sugar that can add up to calories... 50 to a quarter cup!

The lower-growing Pirie and Hayden mango trees are more suited to smaller gardens as the fruit is more accessible and flavorful. Although these varieties have been used in making chutney, they can't begin to compare with the common mangoes for chutney as they are starchy when green.

It's simple to freeze an oversupply of mangoes to use later in preserves, pies, cakes or breads, but don't keep them for more than six months in the freezer.

To freeze mangoes: carefully pick firm, ripe mangoes and use only those free from stings or bruises. Cut off the tough stem end, peel and cut thick cheeks from each side or cut in slices, avoiding the strings, if possible.

There are several schools of thought on the method of freezing. I have had great success in just storing sliced mangoes in freezer bags. Another school recommends making a syrup of 1-1/4 cups sugar and 2 cups water, and pouring the cooled syrup into a carton, then slicing mangoes directly into it. Be sure to leave 1/2-inch head space, before sealing and labeling. Instead of the syrup, substitute orange juice. It is always best to freeze no more than 2 cups of mangoes at a time. Thaw them in the container and add partly thawed at the last minute to salads or compotes for a better texture. Puree riper mangoes in a blender or chop coarsely and bag them separately in ziplock bags to use later for slushes, sauce for ice cream, baked goods and even a delicious soup.

Fully matured green mangoes are perfect for pickling, seeds and chutney. Mango sauce is best made with half-ripe mangoes and has been likened to making apple sauce. Just peel and slice mangoes into a pot, cover with water and add sugar according to the sweetness of the mangoes or to taste. While cooking, stir frequently and add more water if it becomes too thick. Optional: add lemon juice, cinnamon or nutmeg to taste.

One of the most beautiful rooms in a *kama'aina* home was paneled in light mango wood, and bowls and dishes made of the same wood are handsome pieces in great demand.

When mangoes are plentiful, it's a good time to bring out the dehydrator and make dried mango slices. Peel and cut pieces uniformly… about an eighth of an inch… and place on racks in the dehydrator. Shift racks a few times and leave until the slices are fully dried.

For a delicious salad, combine bite-sized pieces of ripe mangoes with chopped watercress and slices of avocado. Toss with your favorite French dressing.

When making deviled eggs, add a bit of powdered ginger, salt and curry to the yolk to taste and mash with mayonnaise. Fill the whites and top with mango chutney, chopped macadamia nuts and a sprig of parsley for garnish.

For a tasty dip, in the middle of a platter of sliced apples, pears, or peaches, blend a cup of sliced mangoes until smooth. Beat one softened 3-ounce package of cream cheese until smooth, then blend in the mangoes, 1 cup sour cream, 3/4 teaspoon lime juice and blend. Chill and serve.

Before adding custard to cups, line bottom with sliced mangoes.

To jazz up a can of Spam, top with slices of mangoes and sprinkle a mixture of 1/4 cup brown sugar, 2 tablespoons butter and 1 teaspoon curry over Spam and mangoes. Broil until it heats and mangoes bubble.

Or you can substitute slices of ham.

Steep 1 cup sliced mangoes in 1/2 cup rum until well marinated, then blend into a softened quart of vanilla ice cream and freeze. Or top an Angel Food Cake with the slices and add some whipped cream!

Spice up your Chicken Salad with the following mixture: combine 1 cup mayonnaise with 1/4 cup chopped mango chutney, 2 tablespoons lemon juice and a dash of cayenne pepper. Whirl in blender briefly. Serve the salad on a bed of lettuce and surround this with sliced mangoes.

Make an easy but tempting salad by slicing mangoes onto a bed of lettuce and adding a scoop of cottage cheese.

Frost a small block of cream cheese with chopped mango chutney, garnish with parsley and serve with crackers for a *pupu*.

Add slices of chilled mangoes to your dry cereal for a treat.

CHUTNEY #1 (MY FAVORITE CHUTNEY RECIPE!)

12 c mangoes	4 teaspoons allspice
3 c vinegar	2 teaspoons ground cloves
12 c brown sugar	2 teaspoons nutmeg
2 large onions, chopped	4 or 5 small red Hawaiian chili peppers,
1 large whole garlic, chopped	seeded and chopped coarse
1 package seedless raisins, chopped	Hawaiian salt
1/2 c fresh ginger, slivered	2 c macadamia nuts, chopped (optional)

Peel mangoes, cut in 1-1/2-inch cubes or slices and sprinkle with Hawaiian salt. Let stand overnight.

Rinse mangoes. Tie spices loosely in cloth bag.

Boil sugar, vinegar and spice bag for 1/2 hour, add onions, fresh ginger, garlic, peppers, and raisins. Add half the mangoes, simmer for 1/2 hour. Add the rest of the mangoes, and nuts. Simmer for about 2 hours, stirring often. Mangoes should be transparent when done. Pour in jars, seal with paraffin.

MANGO CHUTNEY

2 c vinegar	3 c seedless raisins, chopped
5-1/2 c sugar, mill or white sugar	2 large onions, chopped
10 c green common mangoes, sliced	1/2 c fresh orange peel, finely sliced
1 teaspoon Hawaiian salt	2/3 c blanched chopped almonds
1/2 c green ginger, chopped	or macadamia nuts, (optional)
4 cloves garlic, chopped fine	
4 red chili peppers, seeds removed and chopped	

Sprinkle a small handful of Hawaiian salt over the mangoes, mix thoroughly and leave on the counter for at least 3 hours. Rinse well.

Boil vinegar and sugar for about 10 minutes, add one-half the mangoes and the rest of the ingredients except the nuts. Mix well, bring to a boil and continue cooking over medium heat, stirring frequently, for 1/2 hour. Then add the rest of the mangoes and nuts. Cook another hour until thick... remember to stir! Ladle into sterilized jars, pour paraffin over the top, seal and label with the date.

Sweet Mango Relish

1 qt. green mangoes, chopped	1 c vinegar
2 large onions, chopped	4 c sugar
6 sweet red peppers, chopped	1 tablespoon Hawaiian salt
2 large hot peppers, de-seeded and chopped	1 tablespoon mustard seed
	1 tablespoon celery seed

Combine all ingredients, bring to a boil and boil for 10 minutes. Let stand overnight. Next morning cook until slightly thickened. Jar and seal.

Pickled Mangoes

Boil together for 5 to 10 minutes 1-1/2 cups vinegar, 3 cups sugar, 1 teaspoon whole cloves and 1 stick cinnamon broken in half. Add 2 quarts sliced green mangoes, bring to a boil and boil gently for 20 to 30 minutes. Remove cinnamon and jar. Let this stand in the refrigerator several days if possible. If you like it red, just add red coloring!

Sweet Mango Pickle

1 large green mango, peeled and sliced	5 cloves
1 c brown sugar	3 peppercorns
1/2 c water	cinnamon to taste
1/2 c vinegar	1/4 bay leaf

Make a syrup of everything except the mango and boil for 5 minutes. Add mango slices and cook until tender. Fill tall jars with the mixture to within 1 inch of the top. Add plain boiled water to within 1/4 inch of the top and seal.

Carla's Mango-Macadamia Nut Bread is rich and moist

Cream 1/2 cup butter with 1 cup sugar until frothy and add 2 beaten eggs. Purée 1-1/2 cups mango with juice of 1/2 lemon or lime and add to mixture, blending well.

Combine and fold in 2 cups flour sifted with 3 teaspoons baking powder, 1 teaspoon cinnamon, 1 teaspoon nutmeg, 1/2 teaspoon salt and blend well.

Add 1 cup chopped macadamia nuts, pour into a loaf pan and bake in 350° oven for 1 hour and test toothpick in middle to come out clean.

This bread is rich and moist, and you may triple the recipe and make five 7x3x2-inch aluminum pans and freeze.

Mango Shortbread

Cream 1-1/2 cups butter with 1 cup sugar until fluffy. Add 4 cups sifted flour. Press half of above mixture into greased 9x13-inch pan.

Mix:

4 c sliced mangoes	1-1/2 teaspoons cinnamon
1/2 c sugar	dash of nutmeg if desired
1/4 c flour	

Pour mixture over dough and crumble other half of dough over fruit mixture. Bake in 350 oven for 1 hour.

Haupia Mango Pie

1 prepared graham cracker crust   1 cup thawed coconut cream
1 package Haupia Pudding Mix   sliced mangoes

Make *haupia* according to directions on the package. Substitute only 1 cup of coconut milk for a cup of water. When thickened, pour into prepared pie crust, place in refrigerator to cool and set.

When set, top with as many sliced mangoes as you like. Cover with saran wrap and leave in refrigerator until ready to serve. You may either frost the pie with whipped cream or serve the pie with ice cream.

Mango Upside Down Cake

Add 2 tablespoons lemon juice to 2 c sliced mangoes.

Melt 1 tablespoon oleo in an 8 inch cake pan, add 1/3 cup brown sugar and place mangoes on top and set aside.

Whip up a box of yellow cake mix according to directions and pour over mangoes. Bake in 375° oven for about an hour, or until toothpick inserted in the middle comes out dry. Remove from oven and turn upside down on serving plate.

Crunchy Top Mango Pie

1 9" unbaked pie crust   1 egg yolk

Brush crust with yolk and preheat oven to 400°.

Filling: Toss 4 heaping cups fresh sliced mangoes with 2 tablespoons flour, 1/2 teaspoon cinnamon and a couple of dashes of nutmeg until they are evenly coated. Drizzle over juice from 1 large lemon and 1/4 cup honey. Mix gently.

Topping: Combine and mix well: 2 cups raw rolled oats, 5 tablespoons butter and 3 tablespoons honey melted together, 1/2 teaspoon cinnamon, 1/2 cup chopped almonds and 1/4 cup flour, mixed with 1/2 teaspoon salt.

Pour mango filling into crust. Sprinkle oat mixture evenly over mangoes and pat firmly into place. Bake 35 to 45 minutes in 400° oven turned down to 375° after the first 10 minutes. If the top begins to brown too quickly, cover the pie with foil. Serve warm or cold, with or without whipped cream.

Cold Mango Bisque

Puree 3 cups of mango and blend with 5 cups yogurt and 1 cup heavy cream or 6 cups iced milk, 2 tablespoons vanilla, and add passion fruit to taste and consistency. Refrigerate and serve very cold. If you like the taste of ginger, add grated ginger to taste.

Serve very cold in crystal bowls or cups to appreciate the color. It is a rich soup, so serve a light salad or soufflé with it.

Chicken with Mangoes

Place needed amount of deboned and skinned chicken breast in large casserole and season with salt and pepper. Cover completely with sliced mangoes and pour one can of cream of mushroom soup seasoned with curry over chicken to taste. Bake at 325° for 1 hour. Serve hot with rice.

The reason mangoes are the verboten fruit to take to the mainland is that Hawai'i's fruits and vegetables are infested with fruit fly eggs and larvae and the weevil lodges in the mango seed.

Mango Mousse

Coarsely purée 4 to 6 cups mangoes, add 1 cup sugar, juice of 1 lemon and a jigger of Triple Sec. Mix thoroughly and let stand at room temperature.

Mix three envelopes gelatin in 1/2 cup cold water and dissolve evenly over very low heat. Pour gelatin mixture into mango mix and stir well. Chill thoroughly.

Whip 3 cups heavy cream, chill and then fold into mango mixture.

Pour into a tubular mold or dessert bowl and chill for at least 1 hour or more. To serve, unmold and fill center with chopped mangoes or serve from bowl with chopped mangoes on the side.

Mountain Apple

The mountain apple tree, or *'ohi'a-'ai*, as the old Hawaiians called it, grows wild in rainy, shady valleys, but can be a great addition to one's gardens because of its colorful showing during its different stages of the year. The small tree with shiny leaves sprouts feathery magenta blossoms on the trunk in spring and heralds a summer crop of the refreshing fruit.

The fruit's thin, transparent skin turns from shades of greenish white to pink and finally to a deep, shiny magenta. The crisp white flesh around a brown seed has a delicious flavor and is best eaten dead ripe. Unfortunately, the mountain apple does not contain enough pectin for jams and jellies.

We have a tree that gives us much pleasure with its vivid greens and reds besides luscious fruit to munch on. After the blooming season, the ground below is covered with small sprouting seedlings from the fruit that has dropped.

Mountain apples remind me of our youthful summer days of hiking up to Sacred Falls in Hau'ula Valley to gather guavas and yellow ginger. There were always mountain apples to quench our thirst and the lovely pool at the head of the valley to cool off under the tumbling waterfall. Religiously, we always followed one of the valley's traditions by replacing old leaves placed under rocks by preceding hikers with fresh 'ohia leaves to insure a safe trip.

Since the skin is edible, slices of mountain apple are a colorful and delicate-tasting addition to fruit salads and fruit compotes.

Try slices of mountain apple in lemonade.

Or instead of an apple pie try a mountain apple pie.

Line the pan with a pastry and fill generously with sliced mountain apple. Sprinkle over 1/2 cup sugar, bits of butter, juice of half a lemon and bake in 350° oven for 15 minutes. Then cover the fruit with strips of pastry to form a lattice effect and bake until the crust browns.

For Mountain Apple Pickle, combine 1 pint vinegar and 3 pounds sugar and season with one part cloves and two parts cinnamon. Bring to a boil, drop in whole, halved or quartered seeded fruit and cook for 30 minutes or until fruit is translucent and still crunchy. Pack some fruit in sterilized jars and completely cover with syrup then seal.

Super Mountain Apple Pie

Combine 4 cups sliced mountain apples, 1/2 teaspoon salt, 1 teaspoon each cinnamon and nutmeg, 1 cup white sugar, 3 tablespoons melted butter and juice from 1 lemon.

Cook and stir until mountain apples are half done and add 3 tablespoons tapioca. Cool. Pour this into unbaked pie crust and bake in 375° oven for about 40 to 50 minutes. Enjoy while still warm with whipped cream or ice cream.

Unfortunately, gone are the days when 'family-style road-side stands' displayed plates stacked with pyramids of mountain apples.

Nioi

The small, colorful, innocent-looking *nioi*, or chili pepper, is the hottest thing that's been around in Hawai'i since 1815, and so hot that no one really wants to have too much to do with it and many people don't even really appreciate its full potential!

All self-respecting, self-preserving kids growing up in the Islands were taught to have a great respect for the sea… and the little bush that grew wild in most gardens. Its small, shiny, narrow, inch-long fruit, thicker at the stem and roughly pointed at the end, vary in shades from green, yellow and orange to red. Ordinarily peppers grow hanging down, but this fruit sticks up!

As kids grew older and more daring, they ventured to shake a few drops of the reddish liquid over their *kaukau* from the recycled Worcestershire bottle that always graced the dining room table along with the salt and pepper shakers. Before they realized it, they had reached maturity and become addicted to Chili Pepper Water! It did wonders to jazz up some disliked vegetables, too. If you tried to 'show off' and sprinkle your steak too generously with the sauce, you could always ease the pain with a few generous spoonfuls of poi or rice… but not stem the teary eyes!

Unfortunately, today that popular little *kama'aina* bush isn't found in too many home gardens. A pity, really, because like herbs growing outside a kitchen door, the *nioi* can be added to so many dishes for flavor, and is a must in making chutney.

However, some smart people have found that they make attractive and practical potted plants and keep a bush handy at all times. You can usually find plants or loose peppers at the Farmers' Market or packaged *nioi* at Hawaiian food stalls. The peppers freeze well in ziplock bags.

Actually, children of all races and creeds were familiar with the chili pepper. The old-time Hawaiians didn't think *pulehu*'ed steaks tasted like anything unless marinated in soy sauce combined with slices of ginger, garlic and lots of chopped *nioi* before grilling.

The Koreans used it generously in their Kim Chee and for seasoning their meats. The Portuguese Vindha d'Alhos wasn't all that good unless the chili pepper dominated the taste of vinegar, salt and garlic.

Universally, the bottle of chili pepper water was a must on every *kama'aina* table. The best container was an old Worcestershire bottle, as you could control the flow but a ketchup or vinegar bottle or even an elegant crystal bottle etched with the word 'bitters' in silver served the same purpose.

The contents varied, too. The basic recipe, though, was to almost fill a sterilized bottle with cooled boiled water, add salt to taste and add any amount of slightly crushed, washed and stemmed peppers and keep refrigerated. If you don't want it all that hot, don't crush the peppers but put them in whole with stems removed. If you prefer to use gin, vodka, or vinegar, just fill the bottle half full with peppers, crushed or whole, and add liquid to fill container.

If you love garlic, add a few chopped cloves to the bottle.

Add some chopped chilis to your barbecue sauce of soy, garlic and ginger and your meat will be really seasoned!

Instead of combining the powdered mustard with soy for sashimi, substitute crushed chili pepper instead.

You can even drop a whole *nioi* into simmering stew… but be sure to remove it before serving!

Remember… a chili pepper eaten whole can make a strong man cry!

CHILI PEPPER JELLY

3/4 c bell pepper, 1/2 green
  and 1/2 red, chopped fine
1/4 c hot chili peppers,
  seeded and chopped fine

6 c white sugar
1-1/2 c cider vinegar
1 bottle Certo

Bring peppers, sugar and vinegar to hard boil in 8 quart saucepan. Set aside 15 to 20 minutes, stirring occasionally. Bring to a hard rolling boil for 2 minutes, remove from heat, add Certo. Stir for 5 minutes and skim off scum. Seal in small-sized jars to enjoy.

KOREAN CHICKEN WITH HOT SAUCE

4 lbs. chicken thighs
Sauce:
1/2 c soy
6 tablespoons sugar
1 clove garlic, finely minced

1 green onion, minced
1 chili pepper, minced

Salt chicken to taste, roll in flour and fry until well cooked. Combine all the ingredients for the sauce and pour over chicken. Serve hot over rice.

BARBECUE SHORT RIBS

3 to 4 lbs. lean beef short ribs
1-1/2 c soy
1/4 c packed brown sugar
1 teaspoon sesame seed

1 tablespoon each burgundy red wine,
  oyster sauce and
  crushed red pepper
1/2 teaspoon powdered ginger

Mix all ingredients together and marinate the ribs 2 to 3 hours or overnight, turning occasionally. Grill to desired taste.

When all is said and done, you can get a lot of mileage from one little Hawaiian chili peppah!!!!

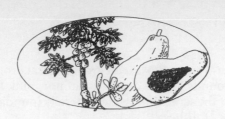

Papaya

Two vivid childhood memories come back at the word papaya... stringing lei from the delicate, creamy-white, fragrant blossoms and being brought up in the Island tradition of having half a papaya with lime for breakfast. Eventually we learned that the flowers were from the male tree and it was the female tree that provided the luscious orange fruit we ate.

In 1919 the Hawai'i Agricultural Experiment Station introduced a new variety, the solo papaya, which produces a hermaphroditic tree that fertilizes itself and bears fruit without requiring a grove of neighbors. Over the years the solo papayas have been improved upon and are sold commercially in the Islands today.

In the more elegant *kama'aina* homes years ago, a dowager speared the end of her halved papaya with a fork and scooped out the flesh with a very shiny silver fruit spoon. Then followed a finger bowl to rinse off any sticky traces from face and hands, which were patted dry with a linen napkin.

In those golden days housewives, or their cooks, tenderized fresh meat by either wrapping it in green papaya leaves and leaving it to stand overnight, or laying the skin or slices of green papaya on the meat and letting it stand for several hours. The old-timers instinctively knew the fruit's valuable digestive properties and that it was full of vitamin A and C especially. The milky juice that flows freely when the fruit is picked contains papain, which resembles pepsin and is used in various medical preparations.

Papaya trees are a very satisfactory tree to grow from purchased seedlings, or you can find papayas you enjoy, save and dry the seeds and plant them in your garden. Papaya is a 'good-for-you' food! So you're smart to have a year round crop in your backyard. The tree grows fast, taking only 10 to 12 months for a black seed to become a sturdy tree with fruit clustered just below the spreading leaves.

The papaya is a sweet, melon-like fruit, round to oblong in shape and 3 to 5 inches in diameter, with a smooth, rather thin skin shading from green in the immature fruits to deep orange-yellow when fully ripe. The flesh varies from pale yellow to deep orange or even deep salmon or watermelon pink in color, and the cavity of the fruit contains many round black, peppery seeds.

We do have a variety whose fruit grow to great proportions, weighing almost 10 pounds, with a delicious salmon-pink flesh. When several come ripe at the same time, we are literally inundated with papaya to try in all sorts of dishes.

Half a small green papaya contains 35 calories, 43 when half-ripe, 78 when ripe. They furnish nearly twice the adult's vitamin C and nearly three-quarters of the vitamin A allowance. Papayas are also a good source of potassium and are low in sodium. Since the papaya increases in vitamin C as it ripens, it's best to use fully ripened fruit.

Select fruit with skin that is unbroken, unbruised and free of signs of deterioration. For immediate use, select fruit that has at least some yellow on the green colored fruit. Leave green fruit on the counter at room temperature until the fruit is more than half-yellow, then refrigerate until ready to use.

Papaya is an amazingly versatile fruit. It is good for breakfast, lunch or dinner and can be used as a dessert, main dish or salad, and makes a healthy snack. Papaya can be used green in soups, cooked as a vegetable or pickled.

Fresh papaya can't be used in desserts or salads made with gelatin because of the enzyme that breaks down protein. However, it does make good drinks, jams, marmalades, yogurt and a variety of baked goods and ices.

Don't try to freeze the whole papaya, but you may freeze the purée or dry slices in the sun or dehydrator.

Papaya, unlike some fruit, does not darken when cut open.

When serving plain papaya, add a slice of lemon or 1/2 of a lime for flavoring.

A half a papaya can be the basis for several delectable dishes.

For a quick salad, fill half of a seeded papaya with cottage cheese and top with mint sherbet.

For an appealing dessert, fill half of a seeded papaya with colorful flavored gelatin, using a bit of lime juice in the liquid. Just before serving, slice some bananas on top and serve with a dollop of yogurt.

Fill the cavity with a seafood or chicken salad and serve on a bed of lettuce or crisp watercress. You may peel the skin or serve as is.

Mix the chicken salad with a Papaya Seed Dressing combined with chopped chutney and a dash of lemon juice to taste.

Or fill peeled papaya halves with your favorite meat or seafood curry and bake in 350° oven just to heat well, and serve on a bed of steaming rice.

For a change, serve baked papaya as a vegetable, especially with curry. Simply cut firm, ripe papayas in half lengthwise, remove seeds and sprinkle each half with 1/2 teaspoon lemon or lime juice, a pat of butter and sprinkle with salt and cinnamon. Place in baking pan with a little water to cover the bottom of the pan and bake in 350° oven for 35 minutes. Serve hot.

For a delightful appetizer, cut bite-sized chunks of papaya and wrap with thinly sliced ham or smoked salmon and spear with a toothpick.

PAPAYA SOUP

2 medium ripe papayas, peeled,
   seeded and sliced
spray or tablespoon of butter
5 cloves garlic, chopped
1 large onion, minced

1 teaspoon fresh ginger juice
1-1/2 c chicken stock
1-1/2 c coconut milk
salt and pepper

Melt butter, or spray pan, add onion and garlic, ginger and papaya. Leave for a few minutes, then add stock and boil for 5 minutes. Cool down and purée in blender. Season with salt and pepper to taste and add coconut milk. Chill to serve cold, or heat but do not let it boil to serve hot. 6 servings.

CHICKEN PAPAYA SOUP

2 chicken breasts
1 tablespoon fresh ginger, minced
4 c water

1 green papaya
dash of salt

Cut boned chicken into 1- to 2-inch pieces and simmer with ginger in water for half an hour. Peel, seed and cut papaya into 1-inch cubes and add to soup and continue to simmer for another half hour or until papaya is tender. Season to taste and serve.

QUICK CHILLED PAPAYA SOUP

For a quick chilled papaya soup, peel, seed and chop three papayas into a blender with a pint of yogurt, add honey, dash of powdered ginger and lemon juice to taste. Blend until smooth. Add enough papaya juice to reach the desired thickness. Chill well and serve cold topped with diced papaya and chopped candied or preserved ginger as garnish. Or substitute *liliko'i* juice for the papaya juice. Optional: add rum to taste.

PAPAYA COCKTAIL

Cut a ripe papaya in half, remove seeds, cut flesh in cubes and marinate in lime or lemon juice. For the sauce combine 1 cup tomato catsup, dash of Tabasco and Worcestershire sauce, 2 tablespoons mayonnaise and add the juice from the fruit. Chill papaya and sauce separately and combine just before serving really cold.

Papaya Seed Dressing

1/2 c sugar

1-1/2 teaspoons salt

1-1/2 teaspoons dry mustard

1/2 c white wine or tarragon vinegar

1/2 c salad oil

half a small onion, chopped

1 tablespoon fresh papaya seeds

Place all dry ingredients and vinegar in blender and blend at low speed for several seconds. Add salad oil and onion and blend thoroughly. Add papaya seeds and blend until seeds are about the size of coarsely ground pepper. Yields 1-1/2 cups.

Papaya Cake

Stew 1 cup very ripe diced papaya with 3 tablespoons water for 20 minutes and set aside.

Sift together:

1 tablespoon baking powder

1/2 tablespoon salt

1/3 teaspoon each cinnamon
    and nutmeat

1/4 teaspoon each mace and ginger

1-1/2 c flour

Cream 1/4 cup shortening and 1 cup sugar until fluffy and add one well beaten egg. Add flour alternately with papaya liquid, fold in 1 tablespoon lemon juice and bake in 325° oven for 45 minutes. Addition of 1/2 cup raisins is optional.

Papaya Marmalade

1 medium papaya, cut in small pieces

2 oranges, cut small with skins

1/2 c water

Let oranges and water stand overnight. Next morning, mix papaya and oranges together and simmer 5 minutes. Add the juice of 1 lemon and measure cup for cup of fruit and sugar. Cook slowly over medium heat, stirring frequently until thickened. Pour into sterilized jars and seal with paraffin and tops.

Pineapple

Some history buffs credit Christopher Columbus with discovering pineapples growing wild on the island of Guadalupe in the Caribbean in 1493. The Indians called the fruit 'nana'.

The Spanish explorers called the fruit 'pina' and brought their discovery back to Europe, where people acclaimed the novelty the 'fruit of kings' because it was so rare and expensive. Europeans termed them 'ananas' and still do. Scientists gave them the scientific name, 'anas comosus,' and so the word became pineapple in the English language!

Don Francisco de Paula Marin is credited with bringing the first pineapples to the Islands in 1813, and the Hawaiians named it 'Halakahiki'... pine from a foreign land. Mark Twain, on a visit to Hawai'i, proclaimed it one of the most delicious fruits in the world.

In the early 1900s James B. Dole, a Harvard graduate from Boston, arrived in the Islands and became a homesteader in the Wahiawa area of O'ahu. He began growing pineapples, and later organized the Hawaiian Pineapple Co.; eventually his small cannery became one of the largest pineapple canneries in the world. The large pineapple atop the building was a Hawaiian landmark, seen for miles around, and a butt for many jokes. We loved to tell unsuspecting tourists that it had to be brought down because it was overripe.

The pineapple has long been regarded as a symbol of hospitality and welcome. There are still traces of carved wooden pineapples over doorways to manor houses on the eastern seaboard. This was the time-honored sign of welcome home to the weary traveler.

Pineapples were shipped to California from Hawai'i during the Gold Rush days, but so much fruit spoiled en route that the idea was abandoned.

In the industry's prime, pineapples grew on all the islands and became a symbol of Hawai'i, along with hula girls, leis and Waikiki Beach. Unlike sugar, the tourists could see the fruit ripening in the fields, enjoy the taste thrill at nearby roadside stalls, and tour the plant where pineapples were canned.

The land we bought on Kaua'i in the early seventies still had the remnants of terraced pineapple fields that had been cultivated by individual pineapple farmers. Although the land had been let go wild, we still could harvest mini-pineapples that were perfect to use for individual salads. Unfortunately the crops soon died out.

In Hawai'i during World War II, the truck drivers in the pineapple fields had a rather cunning system of beating the liquor rationing imposed on the Islands by the military. Driving through the fields, the men searched out full, almost-ripe pineapples, cut off the crowns and very gently, so as not to make holes in the rind, poked and poked at the pulp around the core with a dull knife until mushy. Then they doused the inside with lots of brown mill sugar, replaced the crowns and left them to continue ripening and fermenting in the sun for 3 or 4 days. When the fruit was full of juice, the men picked the pineapples, took them home and bottled the juice. They called it Kikapua juice, the kick with great power, otherwise commonly known as 'good old swipes'!

Even with all this information, no one has been able to satisfy my childhood curiosity of how the pineapple got its crown! However, the crown is very important when buying a pineapple today. We still look for a bright fresh crown that is small and compact, snap the side of the fruit with thumb and fingers and listen for a dull, solid sound to tell us that it's a well-ripened, juicy choice. The color of a sun-ripened pineapple varies from green to golden. If you can smell that delicious pineapple aroma, it should be a good one!

Pineapple's one advantage over most Island fruits is its availability, fresh or canned; it's a tasty fruit that can add sparkle to many a meal. Also, few other fruits are canned in such a variety of sizes and shapes… chunks, round slices, tidbits, crushed and juice. In some instances one size or shape can be substituted for another.

To prepare the fruit: stand the fruit firmly on a cutting board and using a sharp knife, cut off the crown, pare the fruit and remove the eyes. Cut the fruit in wedges, slices or sticks. Refrigerate immediately. I've always rubbed the whole fruit generously with salt (preferably Hawaiian salt), then rinsed it off before slicing. This tends to sweeten the fruit.

Beware of overindulging in fresh pineapple! It is high in acid and can cause a soreness of mouth and throat.

Unfortunately, raw pineapple cannot be used satisfactorily in gelatin dishes, as the enzyme, bromelin, causes the gelatin to liquefy. Substitute canned pineapple in the recipe.

You may use fresh pineapple for jams and pickles, but there is not enough pectin to make jelly.

Low in calories, pineapple is a dieter's delight! Combined with vegetables and fruits, it makes delicious salads high in vitamins.

Place spears of pineapple in a large jar and sprinkle generously with lots of chopped mint. Makes a great treat eaten as is, added to glasses of iced tea or placed on a bed of lettuce leaves with cottage cheese as a salad.

PINEAPPLE PAPAYA JAM

The combination of pineapple and papaya makes a delicious jam. Add some grated ginger for spice if you like ginger.

Combine 2 cups crushed or chopped pineapple, canned or fresh, with 2 cups papaya, 4 cups sugar and 1/4 cup lemon juice. Bring to a boil and cook slowly, stirring to keep from sticking and burning. Watch for the bubbly spurts that can burn you! Bottle in sterilized jars and top with paraffin.

PINEAPPLE IN PORT WINE SYRUP

Skin, slice and core one pineapple and place in following syrup: put finely shredded orange and rind of half a grapefruit in pan with 5 tablespoons of sugar and 1/2 cup each pineapple juice and port wine.

Cook until rind is clear. Remove from stove, add sliced fruit and allow slices to steep and cool in the syrup. Refrigerate and serve cold.

Note: if the pineapple is simmered several minutes after adding to syrup, it will be more flavorful and last longer refrigerated in sterilized jars. Or you may cube instead of slicing the fruit.

PINEAPPLE CABBAGE SALAD

Combine 2 cups shredded cabbage with 1 cup shredded pineapple.

Or use a cup of grated raw carrots with 1-1/2 cups canned or fresh pineapple. Combine with mayonnaise flavored with a little Japanese vinegar and blend well. Serve on crisp lettuce or watercress with chopped peanuts or green peppers for garnish.

Poha

Once upon a time poha bushes grew wild on all the islands and sprouted in the fields and *kama'aina* gardens. If it hadn't been for the prized fruit, the nondescript bush might have been called a pest! However, *kama'aina* cooks hoarded the bountiful supply to make everyone's favorite Poha Jam to spread on hot, buttered biscuits and toast. If there was an overabundance, we had Poha Pie! In the eyes of the young, the dried *poha* hanging on the bush looked like an angel's magic lantern.

Today *poha* is hard to come by, but if you want to plant *poha* in your garden, find enough space to give them, then buy a packet of cape gooseberry seeds and sit back and watch them grow and propagate!

The little yellow flower emerges into a small, round, yellow-green to orange colored fruit, somewhat like a small cherry, enclosed in a thin, cream colored paper-like husk. Husked, the thin, waxy skinned fruit has a juicy pulp filled with many small seeds.

POHA JAM
3 c raw poha, husked and washed
1/4 c water

1 c sugar per each cup cooked poha
1 tablespoon lemon juice (optional)

Place whole fruit in a pot with the water and cook slowly for 30 minutes, stirring often, until there is enough liquid so the fruit won't burn. Remove from stove and let stand overnight or at least several hours.

Measure cooked *poha*, add equal amount of sugar and cook slowly, but this is the tricky time, as this jam requires constant attention. The jam is somewhat sticky and tends to stick to the bottom of the pot and burn so, when the juice thickens slightly or begins to sheet from the spoon, take it off the stove immediately and pour into sterilized jars and seal with paraffin. Do not overcook the mixture as it tends to harden as it sits. Sometimes after overcooking, and even if the jam has been on the shelf for a while, I have emptied the jars into a flat-bottomed pot, added some water and simmered the jam until it is thinner, then rebottled the mixture.

POHA PIE

1 prepared pie crust
poha jam
custard
1 c milk
1 teaspoon butter
1 teaspoon cornstarch,
    dissolved in a little cold milk

2 egg yolks
1/2 teaspoon vanilla flavoring
2 egg whites
1 tablespoon sugar

Pour the jam into the pie shell and spread evenly over bottom.

Heat the milk, butter and egg yolks in a pot over medium heat and stir in the cornstarch mixture slowly when well heated. Keep stirring to thicken, add vanilla. When the custard is cool, pour it over the top of the *poha* jam.

Whip the egg whites, adding sugar, until they hold a peak, then spread the egg whites on top of the custard evenly. Brown slightly in a hot oven and cool. Serve cold.

For a quicker version, spread the top of the jam with a prepared mixture of boxed vanilla instant pudding mix and add some whipped cream to top it off!

Soursop

The rather odd picture of the small, evergreen soursop tree sagging with the burden of its heart-shaped, spiny fruits can always draw a crowd! Unlike the other smooth-skin fruits, the thick, dark-green skin of the soursop is covered with tiny horns or fleshy spikes. The fruit, about 6 to 8 inches long, can weigh anywhere from 1 to 6 pounds.

Shiny black seeds are imbedded in the white cotton-like pulp that has a unique bland-to-acid flavor, somewhat like a mixture of lychee and pineapple. It is a fair source of calcium but good source of vitamin B and C. The tree produces fruit from February to September. After picking the mature fruit, leave it to soften to the touch before using.

To enjoy soursop, just cut the ripened fruit open, break into chunks and remove the seeds to eat as is. Or add small seeded chunks to a fruit salad.

However, the puréed pulp can be frozen, preferably in small quantities, and used in several ways. To make the purée: remove the pulp from the rind in chunks and either squeeze the pulp through several thicknesses of cheesecloth or through a ricer. By first removing the seeds, you'll extract more of the juicy pulp.

The simplest way to enjoy soursop is to heat 2 cups of the purée, add one package mango, strawberry or mixed fruit flavored gelatin and stir until completely dissolved. Turn into four serving bowls and serve with dollops of cream. The color is divine, and you could stretch it to six bowls and top with a little more cream!

SOURSOP MOUSSE

1 tablespoon gelatin
4 tablespoons cold water
2/3 c boiling water
2 c soursop purée
2 c sugar or less according
    to sweetness of fruit

3 tablespoons liliko'i juice
    (add to water to make 2/3 cup)
2 c whipping cream, whipped

Soak gelatin in water for 10 minutes and pour the boiling liquid over, stirring till it is dissolved. Combine gelatin mixture and puree in a pot, add sugar and stir over medium heat until all is blended and dissolved. Set aside to cool in the refrigerator, then fold in the whipped cream. Return to refrigerator to set. 6 to 8 servings.

SOURSOP MOUSSE II

In a pot over low heat combine 20 marshmallows, 1/4 cup water and 2 tablespoons sugar and stir until marshmallows are softened and the mixture is smooth. Cool, then add 1 cup soursop purée and refrigerate until partially congealed. Fold in 1 cup whipped cream and pour into bowls to set in refrigerator until serving. 4 to 6 servings.

Sugar Cane

Years ago, whether the owner was rich or poor, every garden had a few stalks of sugar cane growing in the yard for home consumption, but we kids loved to defy plantation *luna* and the 'threat of jail with only bread and water' by snatching a stalk of cane from the fields!

Somehow, it always tasted sweeter.

Captain Cook recorded sugar cane growing in the Islands in 1778 and anthropologists agree that sugar cane was brought to Hawai'i about a thousand years ago, when voyagers arrived in Hawai'i from other lands to the south. However, the natives didn't make sugar as we know it today; they simply chewed the stalks to satisfy their sweet tooth! Actually, sugar cane was reported to be the reason Hawaiians had such strong teeth. By chewing on the pulp, their gums were massaged and the bristly pulp served as a brush to clean between the teeth.

There is reputed to have been a sugar cane plantation in Manoa on O'ahu in 1825, but it failed two years later. The first successful sugar cane plantation was begun in Koloa on the island of Kaua'i.

The first shipload of Chinese immigrants imported to work in the plantations arrived in 1852 and set the pattern for the thousands of other workers who came to Hawai'i from China, Japan, Puerto Rico, Portugal, the Philippines and other areas. Instead of returning home after a given number of years, many found life so much better in Hawai'i than back in their own homelands that they remained in Hawai'i and were the start of the 'melting pot of Hawai'i.'

Originally, plantations were small towns out in the country… entities to themselves. Workers lived in camps, *luna* and supervisors were provided sizable houses in another section, bachelors fared well in boarding houses, and the manager lived 'like a king' in the big house up on the hill. Everyone worked hard, and there was a common bond of sugar, fishing, gardening, cooking, family and gossip. The automobile was still a rarity, but there was an ample supply of bicycles, horses, donkeys, mules, and your own two feet. Plantation life revolved around the mill and harvesting schedule.

The four social centers were the post office, where you exchanged the news, the tin-roofed movie theatre for diversion, the ball park, tennis courts and the schoolyard, where athletics were encouraged, and the plantation store, which was overly generous in extending credit.

One of the most beloved men on the plantation was the doctor in the small hospital. He devoted long hours to his patients with understanding and compassion, regardless of status or race.

Familiar sounds on the plantation were the mill whistle at the crack of dawn and again in the afternoon at 'pau hana' time, and the whistle of the train as it chugged along the tracks leading from the mill through town and out into the cane fields. By sheer habit, the engineer waved to clusters of children, knowing full well they were just waiting to grab stalks of burned cane as he went slowly by.

Today the sugar cane trains have been replaced by trucks with trailers that go into the fields to retrieve the burned cane and bring it to the mill. The basic sugar-making process hasn't changed much in 150 years, but the machinery has been improved to increase production at the mill. The final product is still the same... raw sugar and molasses.

After planting cuttings of sugar cane, it took two years of TLC, fertilizing, weeding and irrigating for the fields to be ready to harvest.

The cane is burned to reduce the amount of trash going to the mill and bulldozed into windrows to be grabbed up by huge mobile cranes that dump it into enormous canehaul trailers. Incidentally, since the sugar cane field makes such excellent dumping grounds, piles of abandoned TVs, sofas, and car parts, etc., get scooped up along with the ever-present boulders and burned stalks.

The 'debris' is separated in the cleaning plant outside the mill, and the remaining stalks of cane are washed and crushed in the mill to separate the juice from the stalk. The remaining fiber is called bagasse and used for boiler fuel that produces steam for electrical generation and processing. The juice goes into the boiling house, which has been referred to as 'hot as Hades.'

It's the sugar boiler's job to watch over the technical cooking process that produces the sugar crystals and finally spins molasses from a dirty brown syrup into white sugar crystals. The separation process could be compared to a large washing machine going through the spin-dry cycle.

Rain or shine, the burning, grinding and processing goes on from February to Thanksgiving, when the mill shuts down for 8 weeks for maintenance and checking of machinery.

Unfortunately, the sugar industry is suffering severe losses, plantations are being shut down, and a way of life in Hawai'i is slowly dying out. It is sad to see the passing of an institution in Hawai'i.

However, we still need the energy sugar supplies, not to mention the added taste to foods. As all cooks know, there are sugars and there are sugars, which can make all the difference in the cooking or baking process.

Partially refined and washed raw sugar, or turbinado, often is used for coffee and tea and over cereals, besides cooking. This can be found in health food stores and some supermarkets.

The dark brown sugar sold in cardboard boxes has a heavy molasses flavor and is best in gingerbread, mincemeat, baked beans, plum puddings and other full-flavored food.

The golden brown sugar in cartons has a more delicate molasses flavor and is used in baking, making butterscotch, condiments and glazes for ham. Be sure to pack brown sugar down in the measuring cup.

Don't try to substitute confectioners' sugar (the smooth white powder) for granulated (refined white) sugar. It contains cornstarch and can give unpredictable results, especially to cakes.

All sugar should be stored in tightly closed containers to retain natural moisture. If your brown sugar should dry out and become hard, turn it into a pan or bowl, break it up and spread a damp (not wet) tea towel across the top for 3 hours or until it moistens. Then store it in a new container.

Hot Caramel Sauce

1-1/2 c granulated sugar   1 c heavy cream, heated
1/2 c water   1/4 t vanilla

Combine sugar and water and cook, stirring occasionally over low heat until sugar melts. Raise heat and cook until sugar caramelizes and turns a deep mahogany brown. Stand back in case of spattering and slowly pour in cream. Stir over low heat until smooth, then add vanilla. Keep warm and serve. Makes 2 cups.

Cream Cheese Spread

2 tablespoons golden brown sugar   1 tablespoon each
1 3-oz. package cream cheese, softened   grated orange rind and juice

Mix all ingredients until well blended. Refrigerate until ready to serve. Or substitute chopped ginger in syrup for orange.

Fudge

2 c powdered sugar   2 oz. unsweetened chocolate
3-oz. package cream cheese, softened   1/2 c nuts, chopped
1/8 teaspoon vanilla

Gradually stir sugar into cream cheese, add salt and vanilla. Melt chocolate in double boiler, cool slightly and stir into cheese mixture, add nuts and press into a well-greased shallow pan. Chill until firm and cut when set.

Crystallized Nuts

Combine 1/2 cup golden brown sugar, 1/4 cup cream, 1 tablespoon butter, 1/2 teaspoon cinnamon and 1/8 teaspoon salt in a 2-quart saucepan. Bring to a boil over medium heat and continue cooking, stirring constantly until mixture reaches 224°F on candy thermometer or firm ball stage. Remove from heat, add 1 teaspoon vanilla and 2 cups whole blanched almonds. Stir until candy glaze 'grains' on the nuts. Spread on cookie sheet to cool. Makes about 1-1/2 pounds.

Surinam Cherry

The small feathery-leafed Surinam Cherry tree with its abundance of fruit thrived in *kama'aina* gardens for years before landscape architects discovered they make a very attractive hedge and ornamental tree.

Our Surinam Cherry tree grows down in the bottom of our garden where it can grow wild, and what fruit we don't gather for our favorite tart jam can drop and sprout seedlings to share.

The tree, with its small, eight-ribbed fruit, about an inch long, with colors turning from green to yellow, orange, bright red and when really ripe to ruby red, is a rainbow of colors from March to early May. The fruit somewhat resembles a small cherry in that the flesh clings to a stony pit, but it certainly isn't sweet! It's very acidy and a good source of calcium.

The fruit can be frozen and still retain its color.

The juice combines well with other fruit juices and adds a delightful color.

For basic concentrated juice or purée: wash fruit, remove stems and blossom ends, add enough water to barely cover and mash down. Simmer gently until well cooked, about 30 minutes.

If you want a clear juice, drain the pulp in a jelly bag, but don't be impatient and squeeze the bag! Just let it drip.

Jelly: Measure 3 cups juice into flat-bottomed pot, add 3 cups sugar and stir well. Boil over high heat until jelly sheets from spoon. Remove from heat, skim off foam and pour into sterilized jars.

Put the pulp remaining in the bag through a ricer to remove seeds and skins and make jam with the clear purée… cup for cup of sugar.

Jelly/jam: Boil whole ripe fruit with a minimum of water to barely cover for about 30 minutes, then purée through a ricer. Measure cup of purée for cup of sugar and boil gently until it jells by sheeting off the spoon. Pour into sterilized jars and enjoy! This jam is on the tart side and goes especially well with cold meats.

Surinam Cherry Punch

1-1/8 c cherry juice
4-1/2 c water

3 tablespoons lemon juice
1-1/3 c sugar

Combine ingredients and serve over cracked ice. Or you may substitute club soda for the water at the last minute.

Surinam Cherry Chiffon Pie

1 prepared pie crust
1 tablespoon unflavored gelatin
1/4 c cold cherry juice,
    diluted with half water
4 eggs, separated

1 c sugar
1/2 c Surinam cherry juice
1/2 teaspoon salt
whipped cream (optional)

Soften gelatin in the 1/4 cup of half water and half juice. Beat yolks and add 1/2 cup sugar, juice and salt. Cook over medium heat in a double boiler until thick, stirring constantly. Add softened gelatin and stir thoroughly. Cool. Beat whites until frothy and gradually beat in remaining 1/2 cup sugar and beat until mixture holds soft peaks. Fold into cooled egg yolk mixture and fill baked pie shell. Chill. Top with whipped cream. Optional: either decorate the top of the pie with pitted cherry halves or add them to the egg mixture.

Sweet Potato

During World War II, Hawai'i quickly adjusted to radical changes that affected most everyone's complacent lives… early curfews, blackouts, toting cumbersome gas masks, gas and liquor rationing, Victory Gardens and bomb shelters. The latter were hastily dug in backyards and the unattractive pile of leftover dirt just left in raw mounds was quickly covered with something useful. In most cases, sprawling sweet potato vines that grew quickly, didn't need much care or watering and could be harvested in 3 to 6 months after planting. The tubers, ranging in color from white to pale yellow and purple, were easy to cook either steamed, baked or boiled, in their jackets, and were a favorite of most everyone.

The sweet potato, a member of the morning glory family, has supposedly been cultivated in Hawai'i since about A.D. 1000, and was probably brought here with the taro and other edible plants in the earliest migrations to these Islands. However, sweet potato never quite took the place of the number one taro… except maybe on Ni'ihau, where sweet potatoes and dry-land taro thrived in the arid soil.

The Hawaiians called the tuber 'uala and prepared it in several ways: steamed in their jackets in the imu or grated raw for a pudding mixed with coconut milk, and wrapped in ti leaves to bake in the imu. They also made a sweet potato poi, which unfortunately fermented very quickly and probably led to the discovery of a very strong beer. They also used the young, tender leaves of the sweet potato vines to cook as greens.

Besides cooking, certain varieties and parts of sweet potatoes were used as medicine, and nursing mothers wore a lei of the vine, slightly slit so the milky sap exuded, to guarantee them a good flow of milk. The Hawaiians are still great believers in serving boiled or baked sweet potato to the elderly and invalids.

In the past frugal Hawaiians used old vines and leaves as padding under the floor mats. Fishermen used one variety as bait to attract 'opelu and pigs were commonly fed vines and leaves and tubers for their final fattening before the imu!

Sweet potatoes are an excellent source of vitamin A and provide some vitamin C, thiamin, riboflavin and niacin. They are also a good source of calcium and provide some iron and other minerals. Considered an energy vegetable, sweet potatoes are high in carbohydrates and low in fats and protein.

Unlike white potatoes, sweets have a very high moisture content and do not store well. So buy them only as you need them and use as soon as possible. Keep them in a dry place out of strong light and don't store them in plastic bags. This traps moisture and hastens spoilage.

Today Island fresh sweet potatoes are available for use in a wide variety of dishes at any time of the year. Leftover cooked sweet potatoes are eaten cold, diced into chicken soup, added at the last minute to stir-fry dishes or hash-browned with onions in a bit of olive oil.

Sweet Potato Fritters are delicious as a starch or dessert served with syrup. Boil the potatoes to firm doneness, slice, dip into fritter batter and deep-fry.

Sweet Potato Chips: Pare and thinly slice potatoes crosswise, soak in cold water for 15 minutes and drain thoroughly. Pat with paper towel. Fry in deep fat until potatoes are a delicate brown, drain on absorbent paper and sprinkle with either sugar or salt.

For a simple holiday starch, layer cooked and sliced sweet potatoes alternately with dabs of butter and slices of preferably limes or lemons. Bake in 350° oven until hot and slightly browned.

Another festive holiday dish is simple and delicious. Boil up the sweet potatoes, mash well, add butter and sugar to taste and a tablespoon or more of orange juice to moisten and beat until light. Cut tops off of oranges, scoop out the pulp and stuff oranges with the potato mixture. Bake in 350° oven until browned on top. Or place a marshmallow on top and heat to melt it.

Sweet potatoes seem to go hand in hand with pork at any time.

Koele Palao Sweet Potato Pudding

2-1/2 c fresh or dried coconut, grated   4 tablespoons sugar
 2 c light cream   2 tablespoons butter
4 sweet potatoes

Combine 2 cups of the coconut and the cream in a saucepan and bring to a boil. Remove from heat and soak for 30 minutes. Press all the liquid from the coconut and save the pulp. Boil the potatoes, unpeeled, until they are soft. Peel and mash them and add the coconut cream and the sugar. Beat until light and fluffy. Pour the mixture into a buttered, shallow baking dish and bake in 400° oven for 15 minutes. Melt the butter, add the remaining coconut and sauté for 2 minutes, stirring constantly, or until the coconut is lightly browned. Sprinkle the sautéed coconut on top of the pudding and serve hot or cold.

Guava Glazed Sweet Potatoes

8 medium cooked sweet potatoes, sliced   2 tablespoons butter
1 c guava jelly

Arrange sweet potatoes in single layers in oiled baking dish. Heat jelly and butter to form syrup and dribble one-half over potatoes. Bake in 350° oven for 15 minutes. Turn potatoes and add rest of the syrup and bake another 15 minutes, turning and basting occasionally to obtain a perfect glaze. 8 servings.

Sweet Potato Pie With Coconut

1-1/2 c sweet potatoes, mashed	2 tablespoons molasses
3/4 c sugar	pinch of salt
1 rounded tablespoon flour	1-1/4 c sweet milk
1/4 teaspoon each ginger,	grated coconut
cinnamon and nutmeg	1 prepared pie crust
1 egg, well beaten	

Mix the flour and spices into the sugar and add to the sweet potato with the egg. Dilute with the milk and molasses and pour into pie crust. Sprinkle grated coconut on the top and bake in 350° oven for 30 minutes or until silver knife inserted in the middle comes out clean.

Sweet Potato Salad

4 or 5 sweet potatoes, boiled and diced	1/2 c sour cream or yogurt
1 c chopped celery	1/2 c mayonnaise
1/4 c green onion, chopped	salt and pepper to taste

Combine vegetables and mix mayonnaise with sour cream or yogurt. Combine mixtures, blend well, season and chill well. Sprinkle roasted slivered almonds on the top of the salad to serve.

Sweet Potato Bonbons

3 lbs. sweet potatoes,	1/2 teaspoon orange rind, grated
cooked and peeled	6 marshmallows, cut in half
1/2 c butter, softened	1/3 c butter, melted
1/2 c brown sugar	4 c cornflakes, crushed
1 teaspoon salt	12 pecan halves

Mash potatoes until light and fluffy and no lumps remain. Beat in 1/4 cup butter, sugar, salt and grated orange rind. Let cool and divide into 12 portions.

Press a portion of the potato mixture around each marshmallow half to form an oval shape and coat each with melted butter. Roll in crushed flakes, top with a pecan half and place in lightly greased baking sheet. Bake in 450° oven for 7 to 8 minutes.

Or substitute prunes stuffed with walnut halves for the marshmallows.

Sweet Potato Poi or Poi Palau

1-1/2 qts. sweet potatoes, mashed	2 tablespoons sugar
1-1/2 c coconut milk	1 teaspoon salt

Boil, skin and mash potatoes until there are no lumps, add coconut milk to hot potato, then sugar and salt. Mix well and serve in individual bowls. 12 servings.

Cooked Sweet Potato Leaves

You are more likely to find sweet potato leaves at the farmers' markets than at supermarkets.

Wash 1 to 2 pounds sweet potato leaves, cook in 1/2 cup boiling water and barely wilt them… do not overcook them! Drain and serve as spinach.

Taro

In David Malo's book, *Hawaiian Antiquities*, he contends that the origin of taro goes back to a frail child. In the creation legend of Papa and Wakea, the progenitors of the Hawaiian people, their first child was a prematurely born son whom they named Haloa-Naka. The infant did not survive, and they buried him at one end of their house.

There in the same spot a taro plant sprouted, and they called the stem of the strange plant Haloa, the name they gave their second son.

From these bits of legend and myth we can better understand the importance of taro as the Hawaiian staff of life… stem and leaf, sometimes referred to as a sacred plant symbolic of man's growth and divine being.

History tells us that taro, the cherished cargo in the double-hull canoes of the first adventurous settlers of Hawai'i as far back as A.D. 450, was still the staff of life in the Islands when the first European voyagers arrived; and so it has remained the most important of the old Hawaiian food plants today. Although in ancient days there was a wealth of taro varieties, many Hawaiian varieties have since been lost.

In ancient days Hawaiian men were believed to have a spark of divinity and were regarded as the only ones who could handle the taro, *kapu* to women. The men tilled the taro patches and made the poi by pounding the peeled taro that had been steamed in the *imu*. Using a stone pounder on a large wooden board, they produced a stiff dough called *pa'i 'ai*. This thick poi was then stored in a large calabash, sprinkled with water and covered with a ti leaf. Smaller portions were removed as needed and mixed with water. Only then were women allowed to enjoy poi! Poi was never served in small individual bowls, as that was a sign of stinginess and meant that guests were not welcome. Everyone dipped into a large calabash placed in the middle of the table.

During the monarchy period of Hawai'i, the taro leaf was an important design motif in Hawaiian art, symbolic of the origin of the Hawaiian people. Use of the design was restricted to royalty and forbidden to the commoner.

Kamehameha III's vest was heavily embroidered with wires of gold bullion in the taro leaf design, and later the collars and cuffs of the court uniforms were embellished in the same pattern.

A finely engraved scroll of taro leaves runs long the gilt sheath of Kalakaua's court sword, his belt is encircled with taro leaves and the coronation crown bears a circlet of taro leaves.

Panels in the glass doors of Iolani Palace were etched with the taro leaf design, and one of the original palace sofas features a taro leaf design on the frame.

After the missionaries arrived in Hawai'i, it took them quite a while to adjust to the island climate, customs and food, but they soon learned to appreciate the Hawaiian staff of life, poi and taro. Since potatoes had to be shipped from the east around the Horn, this staple starch was soon replaced by taro, served mashed with butter or sliced and fried like potatoes until golden brown.

The missionary women made taro cakes by pounding the cooked taro to the thickness of bread dough, using a little water, kneading well, and molding it into cakes. Some preferred to add egg and milk to the mixture with a pinch of salt. After rolling out the cakes, they cooked them in deep fat or baked them to a crispy brown in the oven. As flour also had to come around the Horn and was usually riddled with weevils by the time it arrived, the families enjoyed their doughnuts made from beaten taro cooked in deep fat.

Taro leaves were cooked like spinach, and if the lu'au leaf was old, they simply folded the leaf under running water and using a sharp knife cut out the heavy veins and boiled the leaves until tender. The drained leaves were chopped and covered with milk, salt and butter and brought just to the boil to serve hot. The milk was used to overcome any bitterness the taro leaf may have had.

Ha-ha, the stems of the inside young taro leaves, were cooked and served on toast with a sauce made of hot milk and butter or just plain bacon fat, rather like asparagus. Before cooking the *ha-ha* of older leaves, the women had to learn to peel off the thin skin of each stalk and boil it in several changes of salted water until tender.

Taro contains a high concentration of calcium oxalate in the form of needle-like crystals that can cause severe itching if the corms and leaves are not properly prepared and cooked.

Three kinds of taro grow in the Islands and are usually found in the markets. The oblong Hawaiian taro corm is covered with a dark, hairy or fibrous bark, and the flesh varies in color from white to gray, pink and purple.

The cylindrical Chinese taro, also called *bun long woo*, is an excellent table taro and makes superior taro chips. Some people prefer this variety because it contains the mildest form of the biting sting and doesn't need extra boiling. The corm has purple flecks running through the gray flesh.

The Japanese variety, the smallest taro of all, belongs to the dasheen group. The tubers of the dasheen or Japanese taro are the size and shape of an egg and resemble the Hawaiian taro with its gray and brown coloring and hairy exterior. The flesh is more like a potato, with a rather dry and mealy texture and can be boiled, fried, creamed, added to soups or stews, but never mashed. Boil in water to cover for about 30 minutes or until tender, peel, add butter, salt and pepper and serve hot. Or slice it and serve with soy.

Once you become adept at cooking taro, you'll want to learn the many uses for it. Select firm and medium-sized corms of Hawaiian taro. To cook: rinse in cold water and scrub with a brush to clean off as much fuzzy hair and dirt as possible. Either boil them whole or cut up, peeled or unpeeled, but place the taro in a large pot and completely cover with water.

Bring the water to a boil, cover and turn to a gentle boil for a half hour, then change the water, cover with new water and continue cooking until the fork test proves it is done, like potatoes. Personally, I like to change the water at least three times to be sure to be rid of all the *mane'o*. Keep adding Hawaiian salt to each change of water.

If boiled unpeeled, let the taro cool a bit then scrape off the outer skin and any impurities. If the recipe calls for mashed taro, mash it with butter, salt and a little water while it is still hot, right in the pot. Cooked taro can be sliced in desired thickness and fried in butter and oil to a crispy brown texture, or baked on a buttered cookie sheet in a 375° oven for 20 to 30 minutes or until brown and crispy. You may leave cooked corms of taro wrapped in the refrigerator for at least a week.

When Christianity and western customs were introduced into the Islands, women were finally allowed to prepare the poi. The mixing of poi was an art; the *tutu* taught the young girls how to knead the poi before adding any water… like kneading dough for bread. By adding only a little water at a time as they mixed by hand, the process could take a good half hour or more. The most important step we remember so vividly was being taught by our grandmother to 'kahi' the poi when *pau* mixing, or washing the side of the bowl clean with wet fingers and sprinkling water over the top so a hard crust couldn't form. Another lesson I learned was to always wet the bowl or calabash before adding the poi so it wouldn't stick.

Raising taro in the muddy patches is still the back-breaking job today as it always has been, but at least you can still buy the poi already prepared in the market. So it would behoove us to encourage and assist in securing farmland and water for taro planters in years to come.

Before World War II, Rice Market in Chinatown was famed for its Hawaiian kaukau, lei, and stalwart Hawaiian men dispensing thick poi from huge barrels. They would plunge their large hands into the barrel and come up with just the right amount to fill the cloth bag, which was then secured with string. The price? Twenty-five cents!

After you mixed that poi with water to the proper consistency, you had to strain it through a strainer, a sort of square yard of crinoline, to remove all the grit and lumps, leaving a smooth paste. (Rinsing out the poi bag and strainer of minute pieces of taro then hanging it on the clothesline was always my job!) Then half the poi was refrigerated and the other half left on the counter to ferment to one's personal preference for sour poi.

Unfortunately the poi sold today is nowhere near the consistency of the olden days, three times the price, doesn't need to be strained, or really sour. As a matter of fact, compared to pre-war poi you could almost call today's production pusillanimous. To people who used no forks or spoons, it was important that the poi be thick enough to lift from the calabash with one finger!

The only way to mix poi is with your hand! Open the bag, fill it with water and, holding it securely closed, loosen the poi from the sides of the bag. Carefully drain out all the water and then slip the contents into a large bowl. Mixing poi today doesn't really take any time at all, as you have to mix in so little water… unless you want soup.

Poi is referred to as one of the most nearly perfect wholesome foods. Because of its small starch grains, poi is easily digested and ideal for babies, the elderly and sick. If you haven't learned to eat poi plain, or even with a sprinkling of Hawaiian salt or something salty, experiment by using it in muffins, cakes, pancakes and as thickening for stews. Some people love to sprinkle sugar over a bowl of poi, add a little milk and enjoy. Poi can be slathered over bee bites to relieve the pain. Use the cooked taro instead of potatoes in stews.

In the olden days the Hawaiians referred to a feast or party as either an *'aha'aina* or *pa'ina*, never a lu'au. Lu'au was something to eat, the tops of the taro that had been wrapped in ti leaves and baked in the *imu* or combined with coconut milk. The story goes that when old-timers passed a dish of lu'au to *haole* guests, the guests came to call the feast itself a lu'au, and the Hawaiians were too polite to correct them.

There are two kinds of taro leaves, those that must have the mid-rib and tips removed before cooking, and the Tahitian taro or Belembe leaves that can be just picked, cleaned and cooked. Tahitian taro is seldom found in the market but it is so easy to grow in your own backyard. Just a little patch doesn't take too much watering, is prolific, and there's no stripping of leaf ribs or *mane'o*. Pick the spear-shaped leaves with stems when needed, clean and cook in a little water for about 30 minutes until wilted and tender. Stir occasionally. Chop like regular spinach and add Hawaiian salt and butter if you like, to taste. Or add pieces of chicken with coconut milk for Chicken Luau.

For *Lau lau*: just pick, wash, wrap around pork or chicken, sprinkle with some Hawaiian red salt, wrap in ti leaves and steam 3 to 4 hours.

To cook Hawaiian lu'au leaves, begin with two bundles of leaves which may seem like an awful lot of greens, but when it boils down you really don't have all that much. De-vein the stem and mid-ribs, snap off the ends of the leaves and boil in salted water, changing several times during the hour's cooking. Rinse the leaves before refilling the pot. When leaves are tender, drain well, chop and serve like spinach with coconut milk or butter and salt. As a matter of fact, spinach and lu'au leaves can be interchangeable, especially when you add coconut milk to the spinach.

Luau soup can be made with frozen chopped spinach, too, but the delicate, intriguing flavor of the lu'au leaves is so much better. Make a rather thick white sauce, sautéing finely chopped onions in the butter before adding the flour, then the milk heated with a chicken bouillon cube. When thickened, add the drained and pureed luau leaves laced with coconut cream. This should bring the mixture to a soupy consistency. Top with grated hard boiled egg when serving hot.

SIMPLE CHICKEN LU'AU CASSEROLE

Place 2 lbs skinned and deboned chicken pieces in bottom of a large casserole. Boil up two bunches of prepared lu'au leaves in several changes of water until cooked, chop and place on top of the chicken. Combine one 12-ounce can coconut milk and one can either cream of mushroom or cream of chicken soup and blend well. Pour over the top of chicken and lu'au and bake in 350° oven until bubbly and hot... about 45 minutes. You may substitute chopped spinach for the lu'au leaves, but add a bit more coconut cream for flavor.

This dish calls for either taro cakes or baked bananas.

KANAKA STEW

Brown beef brisket, cubed pork or pieces of chicken over high heat and sprinkle with Hawaiian salt and pepper to taste. Add boiling water to barely cover, add quartered onions and cook 1 hour. Add prepared and cooked lu'au leaves and continue cooking until meat is well done. If you like it hot, add a whole chili pepper, but be sure and remove it before serving! Some like to add slices of ginger while browning the meat.

Taro is one of the most nutritious foods, so serve it often, especially in dishes that call for potatoes. Taro contains nutrients of calcium, iron, thiamin and riboflavin. Taro was one of the main reasons the ancient Hawaiians had such strong bone structure, good skin and teeth. In 1900 Dr. John Whitney, a turn-of-the-century dentist in Honolulu, was lowered to the floor of Nu'uanu Pali to examine the skeletons of defeated warriors of the great battle. He found their teeth to be cavity free in most cases! From my own experience I believe that eating even just plain cold, sliced, cooked taro has great healing power when recovering from any illness.

Plain cubed cooked taro is delicious served with a ti leaf-covered platter of *kalua*-style pork with a dish of Hawaiian salt. It's simple and popular.

Basic Taro Cakes

1 medium taro	Optional:
1 teaspoon salt	soy, Worcestershire,
3 tablespoons butter	touch of sugar, dash of Tabasco

Peel and quarter taro and boil in several changes of water with Hawaiian salt until tender and almost mushy. Mash, add butter and a little water to make a firm dough. Scoop out teaspoons of the mixture or form patties or balls the size of golf balls with wet hands and place on buttered cookie sheet. Cover with saran wrap, place in freezer, and put in ziplock bags when frozen. When ready to use, bake directly from the freezer at 450° for 30 minutes or until nicely browned. Should make about 30 balls.

For a snappy pupu, add crumbled Portuguese sausage and chopped green onions.

Taro Corned Beef Hash Pupu

3 c taro, cooked and mashed	2 eggs
1 medium round onion,	1 c corned beef
chopped or use green	salt and pepper to taste

Mix ingredients, pat to small ball size and pan-fry till brown.

Washington Place Taro Cakes

(from a recipe during Gov. Lawrence Judd's term in office)

1 teaspoon baking powder	1/4 teaspoon salt
1 tablespoon sugar	1 c hot boiled taro, mashed

If mixed when hot, add no water and put in small greased muffin pans, pat level, make indentation and add a dab of butter. Bake in hot oven for 30 minutes at 350° until puffy and brown.

Baked Taro Puffs

2 tablespoons baking powder	1/2 c flour
1 teaspoon salt	2 c taro, mashed

Sift dry ingredients and work into mashed taro with hands. Shape into balls and place each ball on small buttered muffin tin about two-thirds full. Press a small lump of butter into the top of each ball and bake in 475° oven for 10 to 15 minutes until they puff up and brown. Serve immediately with butter, and guava jelly is nice, too.

Taro Pancakes Chinese Style

1 tablespoon oil	2 c Bisquick
1 lup chong, chopped	1 teaspoon salt
1/2 c char siu, chopped	2 c water
1/2 c Chinese parsley, chopped	1/2 c ham or Spam, chopped
2 c cooked taro, diced	

Heat oil in skillet and fry lup chong lightly for 2 minutes. Add ham and char siu; stir-fry for 2 minutes and remove from heat to stir in green onion, parsley and taro. Set aside. Combine Bisquick, salt, egg and water and beat until smooth. Stir taro mixture into batter. Heat griddle and oil lightly. Drop batter onto griddle and cook until golden brown, turning once. Makes 24 4-inch or 4 dozen *pupu*-sized pancakes.

Poi Muffins

1 c poi	3 teaspoons baking powder
2/3 c buttermilk	1/4 teaspoon baking soda
2 eggs	3 tablespoons sugar
1/3 c oil	1/2 teaspoon salt
2 c flour	

Combine first 4 ingredients; combine dry ingredients and mix together until moistened. Turn into buttered muffin pans and bake in 350° oven for 30 minutes. Serve warm.

Kulolo Taro Pudding

4 ti leaves	1-1/3 c raw sugar
1/3 c coconut milk	2 c raw taro, grated

Line an 8-inch pan with foil and then with ti leaves. Combine taro, milk and sugar, mix well and pour into prepared pan. Cover with ti leaves and cover pan tightly with foil. Steam 5 to 6 hours. Cool and cut into 1-1/3-inch pieces. 16 servings.

Taro and Sweet Potato in Coconut Milk

4 c each taro and sweet potato	2 c coconut milk
cooked and cut in 1-inch cubes	1/3 c sugar

Combine taro and sweet potato in a pot, add coconut milk and sugar and mix well. Let cook for 5 to 10 minutes before serving hot. 6 servings.

Squid and Lu'au With Coconut Cream

After removing the teeth and 'ala'ala (ink bags) from the squid, rinse well and pound vigorously with salt until tender. Boil in 2 cups water and teaspoon salt for 1/2 hour, drain, cut into serving pieces and combine with ample cooked lu'au leaves and add the rich coconut cream (what's left from straining a can of frozen coconut cream). Keep warm to serve, but don't boil.

Today, to keep the coconut milk from souring, combine 1 teaspoon salt with 1/2 cup milk, bring to a boil, let settle then add to pint of frozen coconut.

Taro Chips

Peel raw taro clean and slice thin with slicer. Dry and deep-fry in oil heated to 380°. Drain on paper towels and salt generously. These may be frozen, or stored in air-tight containers.

Cooked Taro Chips

Boil whole unpeeled taro till cooked through. Chill, then slice as thin as possible. Fry in hot oil until crisp, about 10 minutes. Use heavy frying pan or deep fryer. Dry on cake rack, absorbent paper and sprinkle with salt or garlic salt. These can be frozen also.

Watercress

Watercress has been one of the most popular fresh vegetables in the Islands since it grew wild in the streams an 'a'alu, commonly referred to as *awai* by kama'aina in the valley. The Chinese peddlers, bent over from the weight of bamboo poles stretched across their shoulders to balance baskets of fresh watercress and Manoa lettuce, were one of the first neighborhood salesmen. Then came the men in their rickety trucks who arrived right at the back door, tooted the horn and let down the sides of the truck to display fresh vegetables and a few staples. We kids dared one another to 'snitch' stalks of watercress bunched under wet gunnysacks when the old gent wasn't looking and hoped our mom's purchases would cover his loss. Today, of course, you can find watercress conveniently packed in bunches in supermarkets but doubled in price.

Watercress is full of iron, calcium, potassium, sodium and phosphorus, with only four calories per ounce, and packs a vitamin punch of A, C, B, and G. Spring and artesian well water play a prominent role in the production of Hawaiian watercress. Since watercress receives its nutrients through the water in which it grows, it must be planted in an area where the water is pure enough for drinking!

This dark-green vegetable with its tangy flavor is delicious not only just to nibble on but it adds spice to such a variety of dishes ranging from dainty English tea sandwiches and tasty soups to sukiyaki, and is interchangeable with lettuce for salads and garnish.

Chopped in 1-inch lengths, it's great in stir-fry dishes with other vegetables and added to packaged *saimin*.

Mix finely minced watercress with softened cream cheese and season with Tabasco sauce for a delicious sandwich spread.

Chop off the toughest part of the stem end and save this to chop up into soups. It's good for flavoring.

You can always eat it plain as a green vegetable. Just wash a bunch of watercress, discard any old leaves and tough stems and blanch quickly. Chop in 1-1/2-inch lengths and season with either salt or soy and enjoy with rice and fish, especially.

For a quick soup, combine half a bunch of chopped watercress with a can each of cream of mushroom and half-and-half, add curry and seasoning to taste and purée in the blender. Chill thoroughly and serve very cold with sprigs of watercress for garnish.

For a cool salad, combine bite-sized pieces of mango or grapefruit and strawberries with chopped watercress and add your favorite French dressing or honey. If you have pomelo, it's even better than the grapefruit and you don't need the strawberries.

Vegetable Sandwich

1 c cucumber, finely diced
1/4 c radishes, finely sliced
4 tablespoons butter

3 tablespoons mayonnaise
1/4 c watercress, finely chopped

Chill the vegetables well. Cream butter and watercress and spread bread with this mixture and add the vegetables which have been moistened with mayonnaise. Salt and pepper to taste.

Watercress Soup

3/4 pound beef or pork, sliced
6 c water or meat stock

4 c watercress, cut in 1-inch lengths
soy sauce or salt and pepper to taste

Bring meat and liquid to a boil, then simmer until done, about 30 minutes. Add seasoning, simmer about 2 minutes, then add watercress at the last minute so it will be green and crispy.

Creamy Watercress Soup

3 bunches watercress,
  only tender leaves and stems
3 tablespoons butter
1/4 c onion, minced
1-1/2 c water
1 teaspoon salt

1/2 teaspoon white pepper
2 tablespoons flour
2 cans chicken broth
2 c milk
2 egg yolks
1 c heavy cream

Sauté onion in 1 tablespoon butter until golden, add watercress, water, salt, pepper and cook on high for 5 minutes. Puree in blender. Melt 2 tablespoons butter, stir in flour, add broth and milk; bring to boil and stir in watercress mixture. Beat egg yolk with heavy cream. Stir 1 cup of hot mixture into egg and cream mixture then add this combination to soup pot, stirring. Heat but Do Not Boil!

Watercress Pork

1/2 lb. lean pork, cut into small strips
oil for frying
1 teaspoon salt

1 c stock
1 bunch watercress,
  cut into 1-1/2-inch pieces

Fry pork in oil until brown and done. Add salt and, water and when this comes to a boil, add watercress stems. Cook for about 10 minutes and then add the leaves and cook 1 minute longer. Serve immediately with rice.

HAWAIIAN CASSEROLE

1 small avocado, pitted,
  peeled and diced
1/2 c watercress, chopped
salt and grated onion to taste

1 can tuna, drained and crumbled
1 can condensed cream of chicken
  soup, thinned with 1/4 c milk
2 pieces crisp bacon, crumbled

Arrange avocado pieces in casserole dish to serve two. Sprinkle watercress over avocado, season well with salt and grate a little onion over the top. Heat soup and milk, add tuna and bacon and pour into casserole. Top with buttered bread crumbs or crushed potato chips. Bake quickly... 10 minutes... in 450° oven, or broil under moderate heat just until casserole bubbles and is heated all the way through.

Hawai'i-Grown Vegetables

Hawai'i-grown vegetables are every bit as nutritious and flavorful as crops grown on the mainland, and logically much fresher; plus living in Hawai'i, we have a wide variety of choices from the many vegetables introduced by different ethnic groups. Unfortunately, this can become quite confusing as they may be known by several names or by their ethnic names rather than English names, but they are a great addition to our daily menus.

For best results, always choose vegetables that are fresh, tender and young. Most vegetables will retain their crispness and bright colors when stir-fried in oil at a high temperature… a far better method of cooking than boiling.

Boiling is the easiest and most familiar way to cook green vegetables, but there is a tendency to overcook. To keep their fresh color and flavoring, vegetables should be cooked under cover until tender but still slightly crisp. For boiling use lightly salted water, and be sure not to overcook them!

Many of the local produce can be found in supermarkets and at the farmers' markets, where vendors bring in their backyard products to sell. There are a few popular favorites worth mentioning.

Several favorites in the cabbage family include Won Bok, Pak Choi and Kai Choi. Any one of these can be sliced and cooked in *saimin* or sliced raw in salads.

Kai Choi, also known by its Japanese name, *karasena*, is the green mustard cabbage. It is excellent source of vitamin A and is low in calories. It can be eaten raw or cooked and has a definite mustard flavor which adds zest to tossed green salads. It can also be shredded and used as a flavorful bed for sashimi.

Kai Choi As a Vegetable

5 c green mustard cabbage
2 slices bacon
1 tablespoon sugar
1-1/2 tablespoons cornstarch

1/2 teaspoon salt
2 tablespoons vinegar
3/4 c water

Wash and trim cabbage; shred into 1-inch lengths, but keep the stem and leaf portions separate. Fry bacon until crispy, then crumble and set aside. Combine cornstarch, slowly with salt, water and vinegar to make a paste. Cook over low heat for 5 minutes or until cornstarch clears. Add the stems, cover and cook for 3 minutes. Add leafy portion and cook for 5 minutes longer or until crisp and tender. Serve garnished with bacon bits.

Kai Choi and Beef

4 1/2 c green mustard cabbage, sliced
1/4 lb. lean beef,
    thinly sliced 1/8 inch or less
1-1/3 tablespoons soy
1 tablespoon cornstarch

3/4 teaspoon sugar
1 tablespoon peanut or salad oil
1/4 teaspoon salt
1/2 c water

Cut meat into 2-inch squares. Wash cabbage, slice and cut into 2-inch squares. Combine meat, soy, cornstarch, sugar and 1 teaspoon oil. Fry the meat in remaining oil until brown, add cabbage, salt, water and cook for 10 minutes. Serve hot over rice.

Abalone Soup With Mustard Cabbage

3 dried mushrooms
2 qts. stock
1/2 lb. pork, thinly sliced
1 teaspoon ginger juice
1-1/3 teaspoons salt

1 c carrot slices
1/4 lb. mustard cabbage
1 can abalone
6 stalks green onions,
    cut in 3 inch lengths (optional)

Soak mushrooms in hot water, remove stems and sliver. Bring stock to a boil, add mushrooms, pork, ginger juice, seasonings and carrots. Simmer for 20 minutes. Cut mustard cabbage in 1-1/2-inch pieces. Drain and slice abalone, saving the liquid. Add cabbage and abalone liquid to soup; cook, uncovered, until cabbage is tender. Stir in abalone and green onions. Serve hot.

Won Bok or Chinese cabbage is one of the versatile members of the leafy-and-stem vegetable family. You may say it's a cross between romaine lettuce and celery with 8-to 10-inch lovely white to dark-green crepe-like leaves. It has a delicate, sweet taste and can be served either raw or cooked in soups, main dishes and salads.

Just washed and chopped with a French dressing, it makes a crunchy salad.

Buttered Chinese Won Bok

1 lb. Chinese cabbage   1 tablespoon butter
1 teaspoon salt

Wash the cabbage and cut crosswise into 1/2-inch-wide pieces, keeping the tough lower ends separated from the more tender, leafy portions. Combine fat, salt and stem ends of the cabbage in a saucepan. Cover and cook over moderate heat for about 6 minutes, stirring once or twice. Add the leafy portions and cook for 4 to 5 minutes longer, or until leaves are tender, stirring once or twice. Serve hot.

Won Bok Slaw

2 tablespoons sugar   2 tablespoon vinegar
1 teaspoon salt   5 c Won Bok, shredded
3 tablespoons evaporated milk   1/2 to 1 green pepper, chopped

Combine sugar, salt and milk, add vinegar gradually, about 1/2 tablespoon at a time, beating with egg beater after each addition until it is thick. Just before serving, combine the dressing with the cabbage and green pepper. Keep both refrigerated before serving time.

Kim Chee

2 lbs. Won Bok   1 clove garlic, chopped
1/2 c salt   1/2 teaspoon ginger, chopped
1 qt. water   2 tablespoons onions, chopped
2 Hawaiian red chili peppers,   1/2 teaspoon salt
    seeded and chopped   1 tablespoon sugar

Wash cabbage and cut into 1-inch slices; soak in salted water for 1 hour. Wash and drain the cabbage thoroughly. Add remaining ingredients and mix well. Press into a jar, cover and refrigerate. Allow several days for ripening. Serve as a relish. Makes 1 quart.

Won Bok Soup With Meat Balls

1/2 lb. ground pork   2 teaspoons ginger, finely chopped
3/4 teaspoon sesame oil   1 head Won Bok, cut in 2-inch lengths
1/2 teaspoon cornstarch   salt and pepper to taste
1 stalk green onion, finely chopped   1 qt. beef or chicken broth
1/2 teaspoon soy

Combine first six ingredients; then roll into small balls about the size of walnuts. Drop these into boiling broth and cook over low heat until they float to the top. Add Won Bok, season to taste and gently cook until cabbage is tender.

ELEGANT VEGETABLE COMBO

1 bunch watercress

1 head Won Bok

1 package bean sprouts

1 can button mushrooms

1 can miniature corn (optional)

6 lup cheong, Chinese sausage

1 cube butter, melted

Chop cress and Won Bok in 1-1/2-inch pieces and toss in bean sprouts, mushrooms and corn. Add all the vegetables into a large pot of boiling salt water and bring this to a boil. Boil for 2 minutes only, and turn into a colander to drain. Steam lup cheong until cooked and cut in small slices. Turn colander into a shallow bowl so it's a nice mound. Pour butter over and garnish with lup cheong.

Pak Choi, also known as Chinese cabbage, celery cabbage, or by its Japanese name, *makina*, might be compared to a cross between romaine lettuce and celery, with 8-to-10-inch lovely thick, white leaf stems and large, spoon-shaped, dark-green leaves. Slice crosswise, about 1 inch thick at the base and wider at the leafy section. Typical uses of this particular type are in soups using mostly pork, a good stock, mushrooms and flavoring of ginger and salt or soy.

Or steam the chopped leaves briefly and serve either with butter or sesame oil and soy. You might prefer to cook the stalks a little longer than the leaves, so steam them first, then add the leaves. Or stir fry the chopped leaves with meat or other vegetables.

Bean sprouts can be found in the market packaged in plastic bags. Wash these well in a sink full of water so the loose particles and debris may float to the surface and be discarded. These need to be added to any cooked dish at the last minute to retain their crispness or blanched a minute or two when used in salads. Some people like to pinch off the yellow ends.

However, it is a simple procedure to do your own. All you need is a package of mung beans, a quart jar, water and a strainer. In a clean mayonnaise jar add sterilized water and cool, then add 2 tablespoons washed mungo beans and soak overnight. Drain. Rinse the beans, drain, Rinse the beans, drain, return to jar and cover with cheesecloth and leave in dark place... but not so dark you'll forget them!

Repeat process once each day for 3 days and leave on the counter or window sill during the fourth day for greening purposes. Put in bowl of water to remove husks, drain well and refrigerate to keep crisp.

So good in salads or *namasu*, too. Mix them with some chopped ham, green onions sliced fine, salt and pepper and eggs. Drop by spoonfuls and fry like pancakes on hot griddle. Serve with soy and hot mustard.

Combine them in a casserole with thawed and drained French-style string beans, chopped water chestnuts or the Japanese mountain yam or Jerusalem artichokes, can of cream of mushroom soup, lots of Parmesan and top with croutons, canned onion rings and more cheese. Just heat it through till bubbly so it will be still crunchy.

Bean Sprout Salad

Pick over, rinse and blanch 1 package bean sprouts.

Toss with chopped celery, green onion, water chestnuts and shrimp, crab or chicken. Sprinkle soy over to taste. Serve over one thick slice of tomato.

Bean Sprouts Salad No. 2

1 lb. fresh bean sprout	2 tablespoons soy
3 tablespoons scallions	1 tablespoon vodka
or green onions, chopped	1 tablespoon vinegar
2 tablespoons sesame seed oil	

Blanch bean sprouts in a colander and rinse immediately in cold water and drain well. Combine remaining ingredients in a large bowl and marinate bean sprouts in mixture at room temperature for an hour. Refrigerate for at least 3 hours before serving.

Bean Sprouts With Mushrooms, Celery and Chinese Peas

2 tablespoons oil	1/2 c chicken stock
3 stalks celery, sliced diagonally	1 tablespoon soy
1 onion, chopped	1 lb. fresh bean sprouts
1/4 lb. fresh mushrooms, sliced	1 tablespoon cornstarch
1 c Chinese peas, well strung	mixed with 1/4 c water

Add oil to preheated pan and sauté celery, onion, mushrooms and Chinese peas until cooked but still crisp. Add chicken stock and soy and bring to a boil. Add bean sprouts and stir-fry only for about 30 seconds, cover and simmer for 3 seconds. Thicken with cornstarch mixture, a little at a time. Serve immediately.

Chinese peas, also known as snow peas, sugar peas or edible pod peas are sweet and delicious, but they do have strings, and these strings must be removed before enjoying them!! Otherwise you'll be serving a very unpleasant stringy mass. To string them properly, pinch the very tip of the pea to get hold of the string; pull the string up the straighter side towards the stem end. Pinch off the stem and continue pulling the string until there is no more. Or start at the stem end, break or snap it so that you can string both sides at once. It's worth the time!

Blanched sugar peas served with just butter, salt and pepper are a perfect compliment for entrées of curry or pork.

These versatile peas are delicious raw, especially as dippers for cocktail dips; cut or slice them into salads and sandwiches. These peas should be added at the last minute as they require very little cooking and should retain their crispiness and crunch… 2 minutes is enough. They are an excellent addition to Chicken and Long Rice… at the very last minute before serving. They can just steam in the heat of the covered pot.

CHINESE PEAS CASSEROLE

2 c stringed Chinese peas or
    1 package frozen pea pods, boiled
1 can water chestnuts, sliced
2 c fresh bean sprouts,
    blanched and drained well

1 can cream of mushroom soup
1 can onion rings

Boil pea pods for 2 minutes, drain and place in casserole dish. Top with water chestnuts, then a layer of bean sprouts. Cover with soup and bake in 350° oven for 15 minutes. Place onion rings on top and heat again for about 2 or 3 minutes.

STIR-FRIED SNOW PEAS WITH VEGETABLES

6 dried Chinese mushroom caps,
    soaked and sliced
1 lb. fresh snow peas, strung well
1/2 c canned bamboo shoots,
    sliced in strips

1-1/2 teaspoons salt
1/2 teaspoon sugar
2 tablespoons peanut oil

Pour oil into heated wok or 10-inch skillet, swirl it about in the pan and heat for another 30 seconds. Turn the heat down to moderate if the oil begins to smoke. Immediately drop in the mushrooms and bamboo shoots, and stir-fry 2 minutes. Add the snow peas, salt and sugar and then cook, stirring constantly at high heat for about for 2 minutes or until the water evaporates. Serve at once.

The fuzzy soy beans are usually found in the produce or frozen section of the markets packaged or still on the stems at the farmers' markets. However, they are an easy crop to grow and enjoy, too.

Boil the pods in salted water and test one for crunchiness after 10 minutes. Some people like them crunchy, others soft. Either way they can be as addictive as eating peanuts by shelling the beans from the pods. The beans are delicious added to soups and stews, or substituted for lima beans in making succotash.

Serve a bowl of boiled soy beans for *pupu* and see how long they last!!

Plants In the Garden

It's amazing how much of the plant life surrounding us today has been valued for centuries for its inherent medicinal value. Originally the Hawaiians combined the use of herbs for medicinal purposes with strong religious beliefs and ceremony. The Kahuna *la'au lapa'au* was thoroughly trained in the diagnosis of disease and the prescription of different herbs. Hawaiians in general instinctively learned the use of herbs through their elders and prayer. Today this is considered folk medicine.

Fortunately, my grandmother was one who practiced using plants and even weeds from the garden to treat many ailments. I remember her giving someone who had fallen off the roof a bowl of warm water mixed with Hawaiian salt to drink. She credits the *laukahi* plant for saving my grandfather's leg when the doctors told him it had to be amputated. She acted quickly with poultices of *laukahi* throughout the night to drain the poison from the leg and astounded the doctors when he recovered.

The *laukahi* grows close to the ground in the form of a rosette made up of five or six very green, flat leaves definitely marked with one main rib and a few smaller veins on either side. Sometimes there are stalks of tiny white flowers. *Laukahi* is not to be confused with another similar weed which has a much coarser leaf and delicate yellow flowers that tower above the cluster of leaves.

When we were children, our grandmother never used a needle to remove a *kuku* or splinter. She simply found some *laukahi*, washed it, rubbed the leaves together in the palms of her hands to extract the juice, then slapped it over the imbedded foreign matter and wrapped it with clean white rag. The next morning, there was the culprit on the green leaves! Drawn right out with no pain! And so I have treated my children and grandchildren likewise… much to their amazement!

Because of its great drawing powers, grandma also used the leaves as a poultice on boils and infected areas. When she felt tired, she steeped the leaves to brew a cup of tea which she drank as a 'pick-me-up' or tonic.

Recently a malihini visiting us stepped on a *wana* while swimming, and the long black spikes or needles were imbedded in the heel of her foot. I quickly found several clusters of *laukahi* leaves, rubbed them together until there was a lot of juice then slapped the dripping leaves over the black mass in her foot and wrapped it well. The next morning there wasn't a trace of black in her foot.

Another herb or weed I nurture is the *Popolo* or Black Nightshade whose origin in Hawai'i is still obscure, but it was very important to the early Hawaiians. It is easy to spot the *popolo* bush growing amongst the other weeds in the garden as it grows about 6 to 8 inches high, has shiny, small ovate leaves, tiny white flowers and clusters of green berries that turn black. The young shoots and leaves can be eaten raw, cooked or steamed like spinach for its many vitamins.

When I was a child and had a cold, my grandmother found the *popolo* plant, picked a few young leaves and black berries, wrapped them in ti leaves with some Hawaiian salt and baked it. Then I was given the '*popolo laulau*' to cure whatever ailed me! I remember it being very bitter, but it did the trick! She also steeped the leaves in a tea and had us drink that for vitamins.

Recently while visiting the Kilauea lighthouse on Kaua'i, I spotted a healthy *popolo* bush thriving in the midst of lantana clinging to the side of a dry and windy cliff. This can only prove that birds do propagate and *popolo* can survive in very arid areas.

These two plants are amongst several others that are still used by the older folks who appreciate their uses, and more importantly, know how to use them. Today maybe the young have lost interest or respect for our forefather's medicines and should listen to what old-timers have to say before it's too late.

Although I don't profess to have any great knowledge of the use of plants, I do like to think of my garden as being a useful one, too. Pots of aloe sit near the kitchen door so we can quickly apply a peeled leaf of the plant to a bad burn. It heals and prevents any trace of a burn. It can be used for severe sunburn, too. I have also applied the goo from the peeled leaf to the inflamed area when suffering from a bout of gout, and even thought it is quite slimy and smelly, it seems to help.

The green *la'i* or ti leaf is planted in clumps throughout the yard. It played a very important role in the life of the early Hawaiians, and it still does today. We may no longer use the green leaves to thatch our houses or wear as rain coats or sandals, but we continue to use ti leaves on *hukilau* nets to lure the fish, and use them in religious rites, and gifts are still presented in a *puolo* made of ti leaves. The most potent drink, *'okolehao*, was made from the root of the ti plant.

Medicinally it cools the fevered brow or helps to ease a headache when you lay the damp, cool leaf on the affected area.

Two plants I'd like to mention that I keep in the garden, too, for their usefulness are the Achoto trees and lemon grass. We refer to the former as the 'lipstick plant' which old-timers use for coloring in cooking. It's fun to surprise guests with red rice or even pasta! Just dry the pods thoroughly, shake out the seeds, then sprinkle them in a pan with hot oil. Continue stirring until the oil takes on a beautiful red color. Bottle and use in cooking.

We have clumps of lemon grass planted outside the kitchen so we can just grab stalks of this aromatic plant to put in the cavity of a baked chicken. It is known as *takrai* or *sereh* and resembles a leek. You can't miss the pungent essence of the lemon fragrance. It can be crushed and steeped in hot water for tea. Or break off the whole stalk and throw this into a soup pot of stock, chicken parts, raw rice and chunks of ginger to simmer for several hours until it reaches the consistency of gruel. Remove the stalk before serving!

Because of the citronella content in lemon grass, it can be used to keep mosquitoes away on the lanai and smells better than punk!

Definitions of Hawaiian Words

Ahaaina: Hawaiian dinner on a smaller scale than a luau

'Akala: Two endemic raspberries and the timbleberry

Ali'i: Hawaiian royalty

Awai: Small stream

Ehu kai: Sea spray, foam

'Ele'ele: Dark, black; long, filamentous, green, edible seaweeds (enteromorpha prolifera)

'Elepaio: A native variety of taro: the leaves are mottled with white

Haole: Word applied to any white person

Hapai: A native variety of banana with trunk of medium height

Haupia: Coconut pudding served mainly at a luau

Holuku: Mother Hubbard type dress with train

Hukilau: A form of fishing in Hawai'i; to lay a large net to surround fish, then pull it in to shore

Ilima: Small to large native shrubs bearing yellow, orange, greenish, or dull-red flowers

Imu: Pit dug to steam food

Inamona: A condiment made with the cooked kernel of the kukui nut

Kahi: To wipe down the sides of a poi bowl

Kalua: To bake in the ground oven

Kamaaina: A child born of the Islands, a native

Kanaka: Slang term referring to a Hawaiian

Kane: Male

Kapu: Taboo, prohibition, sacredness, forbidden

Kaukau: Food

Kiawe: Algaroba tree

Kukui: Candlenut tree

Kuku: Thorn

Kulolo: Sheer, precipitous

Kupuna Grandparents, old folks

Laukahi: Broad-leafed

Liliko'i: Passion fruit, purple water lemon or purple granadilla

Limu: Seaweed

Lomi-lomi: Massage; to break up into small pieces

Luna: High, upper, above, over, up

Maile: Fragrant green vine made into lei

Mai, mai, hele mai 'ai!: Come and eat!

Makai: Towards the sea

Malihini: Newcomer to the Islands

Mane'o: Itchy

Manoa Lettuce: Locally grown lettuces

Mauka: Towards the mountains

Menehune: Fabled little people who supposedly lived in ancient Hawai'i and came out at night to work miracles

Nioi: Upright, straight

Niu: Coconut

'Ohana: Family, relative

'Ohelo: A small native shrub in the cranberry family

'Ohi'a-'ai: Mountain apple

'Ohia: prized hardwood, from Ohia tree

'Okolehao: Liquor made from Ti root

'Ono: Delicious

'Opae: Small shrimp usually found in flowing streams

'Opala: Rubbish

'Opelu: Variety of fish; scad; excellent dried or eaten raw

'Opihi: Salted and dried abalone from the mainland

Pahu: Hawaiian drum used in the dance

Paina: Small poi supper

Pali: Cliff

Pau: Finished

Pau hana: Finished work

Pilau: Smelly, stink

Pipipi: General name for mollusks

Poha: A Seaweed

Puka: A hole

Pulehu: To broil over coals

Puolo: A holder for lei or food made with ti leaves and tied securely; bundle; usually refers to a package of left-over food taken home after a luau

Pupu: Hors d'oeuvre

Tabu: Forbidden

Tapa: Cloth-like material made from bark

Tutu: Grandmother or elderly lady

Uala: Sweet potato

'Ulu: Breadfruit

Ulu Maika: Stone used in a Hawaiian type bowling game

Wi: Orange fruit tasting like an apple

Index

Notes